ROOTS AND WINGS

Parenting for Stability & Independence

Karen Tui Boyes

Published by Spectrum Education Limited, P O Box 30 818, Lower Hutt, New Zealand

ISBN 978-0-9951314-3-9 (Paperback)
ISBN 978-0-9951314-4-6 (E-book)

Text copyright © Karen Tui Boyes 2021

Designed and typeset by Spectrum Education, New Zealand

All rights reserved. No part of this publication may be reproduced, stored in a retrieval system, or transmitted in any form or by any means (electronic, mechanical, photocopying or otherwise), without the prior written permission of both the copyright owner and the publisher of this book.

DEDICATION

For my parents, Tui and Trevor. You have given me deep roots and strong wings to fly. Thanks. I'm blessed to have you both cheering me on.

For my co-parent, Denny. What a ride it has been! I'm super proud to have walked this journey alongside you.

To Hamish and Sasha – we have given you your roots and wings, and it's your time to fly.

ABOUT THE AUTHOR

Karen Tui Boyes is a champion for Life Long Learning. She is the author of *Creating An Effective Learning Environment*, *Project Genius*, *Your Weekly Gratitude Focus Quote Book*, *Creating The Life of Your Dreams*, and *Study Smart* and the creator of the Teachers Matter Magazine, Teachers Matter Online Summit, Parenting for Resilience, Confidence & Independence Online Summit, Study Smart Boardgame, Study Smart Workshops and the Habits of Mind Bootcamp.

Karen is the CEO of Spectrum Education, Affiliate Director of the Institute for the Habits of Mind, and was awarded NZ Educator of the Year in 2014 & 2017, NZ Speaker of the Year in 2013 & 2019, and NZ Business Woman of the Year in 2001.

A sought after speaker who continually gets rave reviews, Karen has presented in person across six continents, in 20 countries and virtually in 34 countries. She turns the latest educational research into easy-to-implement strategies and techniques. She is extremely passionate about people developing professionally as well as personally.

She is the wife of one and mother of two.

CONTENTS

Dedication   *iii*
About The Author   *v*

Introduction   **1**

Chapter 1. Parenting For Independence   **5**
- Helping around the house   6
- Let them do it   7
- Explicitly teach tasks   8
- Make it fun   9
- Empower your kids by NOT doing it!   10
- Let go of perfectionism   11
- The ability to parent yourself   11
- Praise all efforts   12
- A "pitch-in" mindset   13
- Do it now   13

Chapter 2. The Power of Learning from Mistakes   **15**
- Promoting self worth   17

Chapter 3. Teaching Responsibility   **21**
- What does responsibility mean?   21
- Living the responsibility chart   23
- Ways to promote responsibility   26
- Stop Rescuing   27
- I can't find it!   28
- The inconvenience tax   28
- A hanky, my lunch and lesson plans   28
- A time for kindness   30

Chapter 4. Running With Scissors   **33**
- Fear v's danger   35
- Experiential learning   38
- Learning the hard way   40
- Learning from others   40

Chapter 5.	**Creating Family Traditions**	**43**
	- A month in the front	44
	- Dinner time	45
	- No technology at the table	45
	- Rites of passage	46
	- Pocket money	49
	- Monthly family day	51
	- National Wagging Day	51
	- Friday pizza night	52
Chapter 6.	**School Holiday Challenges**	**55**
	- The no technology challenge	56
	- The Knucklebones (Jacks) challenge	58
	- The gratitude challenge	58
	- The Bucket List challenge	59
	- The clean your room/ice cream challenge	60
Chapter 7.	**Boundaries, Expectations & Rewards**	**63**
	- Punishment versus discipline	66
	- Pick your battles	67
	- Pushing the boundaries	68
	- What will other people think?	70
	- I'll trust you until I can't	71
	- The secret code	72
	- Holding court	72
	- Rewards	73
Chapter 8.	**Setting Your Kids up for Success**	**75**
	- Give them something for the counsellor!	76
	- Ditch self-esteem	77
	- Focus on self-control	78
	- Lessons from Brazil	80
	- Fixed & Growth Mindset	81
	- Praising repeatable behaviours	82
	- I'm going to my room!	83
	- Getting unstuck	83
Chapter 9.	**Self-care and finding you**	**89**
	- Order of importance	90
	- Your glass	90
	- The burnt chop syndrome	91

-	Looking after you	92
-	Your work does not define you	95
-	Designing who you want to be	95
-	Setting yourself up for success	99
-	Morning routine	99
-	The 20/20/20 formula	101

Chapter 10. Maintaining The Relationship With Your Partner — **105**
- The Language of Love — 106
- Connect each day — 108
- Give to get — 109
- I can't mind read! — 110
- The magic fairy — 111

Chapter 11. The Power of Gratitude — **113**
- The benefits of gratitude — 114
- Ways to cultivate gratitude — 115
- Gratitude on the hard days — 115
- The secret of gratitude — 117

Chapter 12. Putting It All Together — **119**
- Set a monthly focused goal — 119
- Everything is hard before it is easy — 121
- The two minute rule — 122
- Final words — 122

BONUS CHAPTER 1 *Supporting Your Teen Through Exam Years* — **127**
BONUS CHAPTER 2 *A Study Session in Action* — **133**

Bibliography — *145*

Appendix 1 Age-Appropriate* Jobs for Kids — *151*
Appendix 2 How to Give and Receive an Apology — *154*
Appendix 3 Questions for around the Table — *157*
Appendix 4 Adult Child Living At Home Contract — *159*
Appendix 5 Extra bits I just wanted to share! — *163*
Appendix 6 Kindness Challenge — *168*
Appendix 7 Holiday Acivity Grid — *169*
Appendix 8 Alternative Questions to ask after school — *170*

Gratitude & Thanks — *171*

Stay in Touch with Karen — *173*

Other Books and Resources by Karen Tui Boyes — *174*

Your children are not your children.
They are the sons and daughters of Life's longing for itself.
They come through you but not from you,
And though they are with you yet they belong not to you.

You may give them your love but not your thoughts,
For they have their own thoughts.
You may house their bodies but not their souls,
For their souls dwell in the house of tomorrow,
which you cannot visit, not even in your dreams.

You may strive to be like them,
but seek not to make them like you.
For life goes not backward nor tarries with yesterday.

You are the bows from which your children
as living arrows are sent forth.
The archer sees the mark upon the path of the infinite,
and He bends you with His might that
His arrows may go swift and far.
Let your bending in the archer's hand be for gladness;

For even as He loves the arrow that flies,
so He loves also the bow that is stable.

Kahlil Gibran

INTRODUCTION

If you are looking for a parenting manual – this is not it! I do not believe one exists. This book is a smorgasbord of ideas, experiences and wisdom I have gained from my 27 years of travelling the world working and talking to parents, teachers and students and, more importantly, my 21 years of being a mum to two amazing souls, Hamish and Sasha.

I also want to get something out front and centre. I want my kids to leave home! I know this is not everyone's goal. I am clear about my parenting role. It is to raise competent, capable, contributing adults. I love my kids and want to see them grow and thrive (and give me grandkids! I'm ready!) They need to leave home for that! I'm also clear that my future happiness and well-being is not tied up in my role as a parent. I am so much more than a mum.

I believe a parent's role is to provide a foundation of stability for our kids. To ground them in great. To create deep roots of confidence and security and always know where home is. Giving your child wings means they can be independent, fly away, experience life, and use what they have learned. Strong knowledge of oneself also provides the impetus for them to impact the world positively. I'm not expecting my children to be Picasso or Oprah, just that they are kind, caring and considerate of themselves, others and the environment, that they leave the world a better place for having been in it.

So, who am I to write a parenting book? I am far from being the perfect parent. I have yelled at my kids, lost the plot, been absent travelling for some of their life, missed birthdays (that our daughter will never let me forget – ever!) and made so many mistakes that there might even be a medal for it!! And that is the point. I have learned so much and am driven to share my and others experiences with you to lighten your load, make the journey more enjoyable and most importantly, not lose yourself in the process.

I did. Lose myself. When our son was three years old and our daughter nine months old, I packed my bags and left my husband, Denny, and kids. It is a shallow place to be when a mother can walk away from her children and husband. As it turned out, I only got as far as the front steps, and Denny pleaded to sit and chat before I left. We sat on those steps and cried, talked and made a plan to take one day at a time. Each night we (I) would re-evaluate my staying or going. I stayed. It wasn't always easy, and together we worked it out.

Looking back, I realise I was suffering from Post Natal Depression. I had two young children, was travelling the country and running two businesses! At the birth of our first child, we had decided Denny would be a stay at home Dad and for me to keep on working. I loved my work. I was (and still am) on a mission to change the education system, and it was financially beneficial for us that I carried on. I breastfeed both kids while travelling, trying to maintain one business while starting another, keeping my relationship going and, and, and something had to give. I had also just been awarded NZ Business Woman of the Year (2001) and thought I was invincible.

Those early years were often challenging, and the children gave me such joy.

Now, 21 years later (I'm sure I'm not old enough to have a 21-year-old son!), there has been a lot of water pass under the bridge. This book is my learnings. The highs and lows, shared with an open heart in the hope that something might spark you to keep going, add more fun and joy into parenting, maintain (or redefine) your identity and purpose, and create a balance in your life that brings you great happiness and delight each day.

So why do I feel I'm qualified to write a parenting book? Because I have walked the journey, made the mistakes, have a thriving 21-year-old son in full-time employment and an 18-year-old daughter who is studying. Neither are sure of what they 'want' for their lives, and I am confident they have the tools and grounding to be confident, capable, contributing adults.

Whether you have toddlers, young children, tweens or teens, there is something for you in this book.

Would I change the journey if I had it over? Sure, I would! I do believe, however, there is no point in dwelling on the could of, would of, should ofs as it will not change what has happened. I have done my best to instil the roots of security and knowledge and the wings to allow them to fly and be independent.

> *The best time to plant a tree is 20 years ago. The second best time is now.*
>
> —Chinese Proverb

CHAPTER 1

PARENTING FOR INDEPENDENCE

> *It's not what you do for your children, but you have taught them to do for themselves that will make them successful human beings.*
>
> -ANN LANDES

During the Christmas break, tragedy struck the young girl next door. Her mother died. It was unexpected. She had been unwell, and the hospital wanted to do an urgent scan and had scheduled it for the following week. She died before that day. The young girl, I'll call her Claire, was 10-years-old and an only child.

What struck me about this tragedy was the lack of independence Claire had. Living only a few doors from the school gates, her Mum had walked her to and from school every day. Every single day of her five years of school. It got me thinking. Many parents do everything for their children, and many children do not know how to do simple tasks.

I'm not suggesting parents plan for an early departure. We, however, do have a responsibility to ensure we assist our children in developing into independent citizens and are ready to leave home when the time is right. I saw a quote once that said, "When your children don't need you anymore, you have done a great job." There will always be times we need or want our parents for support, guidance or companionship, and I believe the quote is about independence. It's about being able to do everyday tasks, at age-appropriate stages, on their own.

It starts early with small steps – having children help you with the daily tasks. Tasks might take longer, and they may even mess it up, which is part of the vital learning process. If your children are older, it is not too late. Chat about the importance of working together as a family, sharing the load, preparing for adulthood.

Parenting for independence is a gradual process, and one that takes time.

Here are some ways to instil your child's independence:

Helping around the house

The research is clear; your child will benefit from helping with jobs in your home. Helping with household tasks builds respect, life skills, teamwork, a strong work ethic, improves planning and time management, and reinforces independence skills.

You will find a list of age-appropriate jobs in Appendix 1. Start slow and ensure your child has mastered each one before adding the next. Some will take longer than others. Be kind and teach them how to do the job correctly. Sweeping the front step by moving the dirt from one side to the other is not OK. Effective sweeping means removing the dirt. They may not stack the dishwasher precisely as you like it, breathe, walk away and leave it – the dishes will still get clean. (If not, you now have a learning point for next time.) I can recall my son folding the towels and being so proud of himself. I just sucked up my OCD and put them away in the cupboard. He was so proud of himself!

Let them do it

It is easy in our hurried busy world to think it is quicker and easier to do yourself. If so, what do your children learn? I love this quote below.

> *If you say it for me,*
> *if you write it for me,*
> *if you draw it for me,*
> *All I learn is that*
> *You are better than me.*
> -UNKNOWN

I saw it on the wall of a classroom many years ago, designed a mini-poster, and placed it on my fridge - both a reminder for myself and our son.

He was two and a half years older than our daughter and was a very proud big brother. (Now it is "Get out of my room!" shouted loud enough for the whole street to hear!) He did everything he could for her as a toddler. He liked to dress her, feed her, get her a drink of water, tie her shoelaces, and he even talked for her. She learned to sit back and let him. This was undermining her development, not that she was worried! The poster served as a reminder for him to allow her to become independent and learn.

Explicitly teach tasks

Just telling or showing your child how to do a task or use an appliance might not be enough. It can take many repetitions for the brain to recall, especially when it is a task they don't want to do. Write out the instructions. I have done this for the washing machine – it saves the huffing and puffing of, "I don't know how to do it!"

> **Washing Machine Instructions**
> 1. Press Power
> 2. Choose wash cycle - regular
> 3. Select wash temp. - cold
> 4. Select water level - auto
> 5. Select spin speed - fast
> 6. Add powder
>   - Full load = 1/2 scoop
>   - Half load =1/4 scoop
> 7. Press start

A reality check I saw once said,

"If your child can use a smartphone, they can use a washing machine, dryer, mop, broom, scrubbing brush, bucket and cleaning products."

We need to teach them how.

Make it fun

Do the tasks together and make it fun. When doing household chores, wear cleaning aprons and scarves. Put on some fun music. Use a timer and small incentive if needed. My teens still love the ice cream challenge! (More about this later.)

Empower your kids by NOT doing it!

What are you doing that your child could be doing for themself? If our children want special snacks in their lunch, they were encouraged to make them. They both became great bakers, and our son is an expert banana cake maker.

From the age of sixteen, they were also responsible for their laundry. If they suddenly had no underwear – tough. It wasn't our job to check anymore. They learned quickly.

You decide what works for you and your family and put the agreements in place.

The fruits of your efforts will pay off. There have been numerous times when Denny or I have realised neither of us would be home to cook dinner. We simply rang the children and asked them to cook the meal. It was on the table when we got home. A healthy, hot meal. It is all about helping out and ensuring they can live independently one day.

As I finish this book, I am away from home in a motel with Denny. He had four days of work in another town, and I went with him to write. Our children were at home, independent and happy (and so are we!) If they choose to eat pizza or get Uber eats for the week, it is up to them. It's their money, and we know they can cook and care for themselves.

Let go of perfectionism

As a parent, you may need to let go of the perfectionist. They will make mistakes. They will not do it to your skill level as they are still learning. Your child did not get up and walk perfectly the first time. It took encouraging words, affirmations, praise and a helping hand to learn to walk. The same is true of all learning, especially if completing tasks independently is a goal. It requires you, as the parent, to be patient, flexible, nurturing, encouraging and forgiving.

The ability to parent yourself

On our daughters seventeenth birthday, I announced I had one year left! One year to ensure she could parent herself. I figured that by the time she was eighteen, she was less likely to be open to parental feedback and coaching. I presented her with a list! It was a list of goals – for both of us – to work towards.

Here was my list:

- To be able to go to bed and sleep at a reasonable time
- To cook for herself
- To make healthy meal decisions
- To be able to make, save and spend money wisely
- To be OK on her own

- To be able to monitor and manage her phone (technology) usage
- To be able to see the needs of others and help out
- Confident to ask for help
- Know how to say no (when faced with peer pressure, alcohol, drugs, boys etc.)
- Be able to deal with disappointment

There are likely to be many other things I had omitted from the list, and even more likely, your plan for your child would be very different. It served as an expectations list, a goal post and a beacon of hope for the following year.

If I had my time over again, I would do this every year – set small, realistic goals for growth and learning.

Praise all efforts

Be sure to praise all efforts and not just the result. It is the actual giving a task a go, taking some small action which is essential. I love the technique of being sure to have your child overhear you telling someone how helpful and independent they are becoming. When children eavesdrop' on a compliment, the positive vibes are felt deeper within themselves. (See chapters 7 and 8 for more information about praise and rewards.)

A "pitch-in" mindset

In her 2016 TED talk, Julie Lythcott-Haims, the former dean of freshmen at Stanford University, cited a Harvard Study spanning over 80 years from 1938 to now. Researchers found a pivotal precursor to professional success in life: having done chores as a kid.

"The earlier you started, the better," Julie continued. "[A] roll-up-your-sleeves- and-pitch-in mindset, a mindset that says, there's some unpleasant work, someone's got to do it, it might as well be me … that that's what gets you ahead in the workplace."

Do it now

>When you've got a job to do,
>Do it now!
>If it's one you wish was through.
>Do it now!
>If you're sure the job's your own,
>Just tackle it alone.
>Don't hem and haw and groan,
>Do it now!

This is the only quote on the wall of my childhood home. It still hangs in the hallway of my parent's house. It is a great philosophy to encourage a 'get it done' mindset.

> *I learn from my mistakes. It's a very painful way to learn, but without pain, as the old saying goes, there's no gain.*
>
> —JOHNNY CASH

CHAPTER 2

THE POWER OF LEARNING FROM MISTAKES

> *When you make a mistake, there are three things you should ever do about it: admit it, learn from it and don't repeat it.*
>
> -Paul Bear Bryant

Coming from a successful school background, with successful parents and being the first person in my entire extended family ever to go to University (a huge deal), my journey was not the plain sailing I imagined it would be.

I loved student life, the freedom, friendships and learning. I was living my childhood dream to become a teacher. Halfway through my first year, I suddenly faced a very unfamiliar situation. I felt alone, humiliated, shamed. I didn't tell anyone from embarrassment and fear of what they might think of me. I failed an Education 101 paper!

Everyone around me seemed to have it easy. They were passing with far less effort than me. This was the first time in my life I could remember feeling like a failure. Maybe the first time I had failed. I didn't know what to do. My foremost thought and concern were, what if my parents found out? They would be so disappointed in me. Maybe they would love me less. I knew they had worked hard to ensure I could follow my dreams, and I had let them down.

What could I do? I had no coping strategies, and I was alone.

At this point, some people may have turned to alcohol, drugs, fast cars, self-harming, sex, anything for some escapism. I choose a different route. In an attempt to pull my grade back up, to save face and make sure no-one would ever know, I cheated. The next assignment just happened to be the same topic set the previous year. I found a student a year ahead of me and asked to borrow her assignment to check I was on the right track. It just happened she has received an 'A' for her work. I copied this assignment word for word. I received an 'A', which brought my total mark for the year to a passing grade – and no-one knew, especially my parents. Except I knew!

I lived in fear for weeks while my paper was being marked, for months before I got the final grade for the year and three years before I was given my degree. What if I was 'found' out? What if

I was expelled from Teachers College and University? What if I was paraded in front of my peers as an example of 'what not to do or be'? What if my parents found out? I have now spoken about this truth over the past ten years in many workshops, keynote speeches, webinars and seminars – and still, my parents did not know.* The fear of making a mistake and not being enough had a firm grip around my throat.

Promoting self worth

The feeling of shame is linked with low self-worth. What I lacked were strategies for dealing with failure. I had a mindset that thought I should be as good as everyone else and believed failing was a bad thing. Allowing your child to fail in the safe confines of your home will enable you to teach them how to deal with failure, disappointment and perhaps regret. Then when they have left home, they will have appropriate coping strategies.

So what can you do as a parent to prepare your child for when they feel like they are not enough and increase their self-worth?

Below is a quick list of ideas

---

* They know now as I had told this story to my children as they were growing up, and at a family dinner, my daughter announced. "Mum, you should tell Nana and Poppa what you did at University!" Cornered and feeling sick, I thought I would vomit (I was in my forties at this stage), I revealed the truth. Both my Mum and Dad just shrugged their shoulders and didn't seem bothered! The relief I felt was immense. I was left wondering why I was so worried and what damage that guilt had done stuck inside my body for so long.

- Talk about your failures and challenging situations and show the growth and lessons learned
- Show your vulnerability so your children know that you take risks, give new ideas a go and make mistakes in the process
- Be authentic – do not pretend all is well when it is not (age and maturity appropriate)
- Show your emotions – it is OK to be sad, mad, nervous, confused, frustrated, and happy, excited, peaceful, hopeful, and full of pride for your accomplishments. This is great role modelling.
- Create an attitude of gratitude. See chapter 11 for more.
- Encourage mistake making and accept it is part of the learning process
- Let go of being a perfectionist and expecting everyone else to be the same (I'm a recovering perfectionist)
- Encourage responsible risk-taking
- Learn something new together – something that takes you way outside your comfort zone, and be a model for learning
- Apologise when you have made a wrong decision, shouted, or acted in a way that you wish you had not. Your child needs to know you make mistakes too. See Appendix 2 on How to Apologise.

- Tell them you love them and back this up with action. This does not mean giving them everything they want. It means holding the boundaries of what is acceptable and what is not.

What would you add to this list?

> *Accept responsibility for your actions. Be accountable for your results. Take ownership of your mistakes.*

CHAPTER 3

TEACHING RESPONSIBILITY

> *If you realise your responsibility, you will realise your destiny.*
>
> -TASNEEM HAMEED

As part of the journey to adulthood, teaching your child to be responsible is essential. I believe taking responsibility for your actions, mistakes, and behaviour is one of the most significant steps to becoming an independent adult. When your child is young, it starts with baby steps and progressively gets more complex.

What does responsibility mean?

Many years ago, I was fortunate enough to attend a series of workshops that changed my outlook and life. The teaching of the 'Responsibility' chart was at the centre of all. This single concept was a game-changer and one I have worked on upholding for twenty-eight years. Here is the chart.

The Line of Life is central to the concept as it shows that there is always a choice in every situation in life. When something goes right or wrong in your life, you can choose to 'play' above or below the line.

Often the default for many people is to BLAME when something goes wrong. We blame our parents, teachers, the government, or ourselves for our mistakes. Next, people will often make EXCUSES. The most common excuse is that they haven't got time. Yes, life can be very hectic, and time is the only resource every person has the same amount of. Everyone has twenty-four hours a day. Next, many people will DENY the outcome. At some level, you just pretend it didn't happen. These three states cause us to become a VICTIM of our life or circumstances. People playing 'below the line' hold pity parties, often moan and whine that life's not fair.

The alternative choice is to play above the Line of Life. When something goes wrong, firstly acknowledge it and take OWNERSHIP. This is as simple (although not that easy at times) as saying "I made a mistake" or "I was wrong." Next is to be ACCOUNTABLE. This means to explain the outcome without blaming or making excuses. It the case of the 'not enough time' scenario, to be accountable would be to recognise that perhaps your time management, planning or expectations within the time frame were inadequate or unrealistic. The next step is to take action to improve your time management. This is what it means to take RESPONSIBILITY. To be response-able. This requires effort to make the situation better or learn from it and change your behaviour, attitudes or beliefs. At this point, you become a LEARNER and can grow and develop from the experience.

Living the responsibility chart

This is harder than it looks and sounds! Here are a couple of ideas and information that may help.

Surround yourself with others who take responsibility for their lives. The people you 'hang out' with make a big difference to your mindset. If people around you are whingers, moaners and are holding frequent pity parties, spend less time with them. Spend more time with people who are living their dreams, inspiring others. Watch TED talks and read personal development books.

It is a courageous person who takes this chart into their life, family and work. If you are willing to point out that others are "living below the line" and encouraging them to take responsibility, you also have to be willing for them to 'call' you on your behaviour. It is often very uncomfortable to see your victim behaviour and have it highlighted. It is, however, a blessing to be able to work through the mistakes and errors to learn and grow.

This is a continual work in progress for all of us. Deep inner work and healing are often required.

An example from my own life is as follows: One of the delights I enjoy is having fresh flowers in my home. I do, however, detest dead flowers! At the time of this story, I had been married to my amazing husband for eighteen years (we are due to celebrate our 25th anniversary next year.) Travelling worldwide to speak at conferences meant I was frequently away. I'd come home from a trip and find the flowers dead in a vase. Petals would be all over the floor and bench, and the water in the vase would smell putrid. I would then go into a rant at Denny. "You knew I was coming home today! You know I hate dead flowers! Couldn't you have thrown them out, wiped the bench and cleaned the vase?"

Denny must have heard this 'lecture' hundreds of times! He always politely listened and nodded. One day, eighteen years into our marriage, I returned home and walked up the stairs when I stopped. I realised there would be dead flowers in the vase! It suddenly dawned on me. Whose problem was it? The truth was that Denny did not see the dead flowers, petals or smell the stinky water. If he did, knowing my total disdain, he would have done something about it!

I walked up the stairs, put the flowers in the rubbish bin, wiped the bench and washed the vase. It took me 90 seconds! There was no aggression, no being a victim, just taking responsibility for my needs. Ninety seconds and he still doesn't know! It wasn't his problem! It was mine.

Many times these lessons just come out of the blue! What really annoys you in your life, and how might you take responsibility for it?

Another example is that I find women's public toilets disgraceful. (Sorry to the fathers reading – I can't comment on the men's room!) Now I can't do anything about the dozens of patrons before me who have left the place so awful. I can, however, ensure the next person who comes along might get a better experience. I pick up the paper on the floor (ensuring I have a paper towel or two in my hand as a barrier) and push it down into the rubbish bin so that many more paper towels can now fit. I also take a couple of paper towels and wipe the bench, basin and taps to make it better for the next person who comes along.

I don't usually tell people about this, as I'm not doing it for public praise. I'm doing it to make the world a slightly improved place for others. Maybe, if it is a more excellent experience for her, she will look after the area better.

Ways to promote responsibility

Start by labelling responsibility when you see it. Each time your child helps, picks up rubbish, fetches something for you, tidies their toys, thank them for being responsible.

When our daughter was two years old, I can recall her setting the table. She called to me from the other side of the table, her eyes peeking about the edge of the table, and she said, "Mummy, am I being 'sponsible?" I smiled and told her she was very responsible.

Another memory is when our children were six and four. I was baking, and they wanted to post a letter they had written to their grandparents. As the oven was on, I could not leave the house, and they wanted to go. The post box was about 400m from our home. They would, however, need to cross the main road using a pedestrian crossing and walk around a corner. I asked them if they could be responsible, to which the reply was a very eager YES! We talked about the road and the crossing and to go there and straight back. I also insisted they held hands! (This was purely for my benefit, as it is so cute, and I know they would not do it much longer.) Off they went without looking back. They held hands all the way there and back - OK, yes, I did sneak out to peek - and both were very proud of themselves once they were back. Again I praised them for their responsibly.

Stop Rescuing

> *I am a lighthouse rather than a lifeboat. I do not rescue, but instead, help others to find their way to shore.*
>
> -UNKNOWN

It is often easy to rescue children when they have learning opportunities, and I have attempted to stand back and allow the lesson to unfold rather than jumping in to be the hero. It's not always easy.

When your child can't find their shoes, give them time to look for them before you run to their rescue. If they didn't complete their tasks, make sure you have a pre-determined consequence and follow through.

I recall a teacher asking parents at a parent-teacher night to ensure we signed the school assigned diary each night. I questioned why. It was not my responsibility to get the homework done - it was my son's. The teacher remarked she had never thought of this. I have never signed a school diary to say I have seen it, and if his homework was not completed on time, I trusted the teacher would have consequences.

I can't find it!

I recall when Miss 14 was cooking a cake for the last day of term at school. She complained she couldn't find the cake tin. I told her it was in the cupboard. Again she said she couldn't find it. She asked me to come and look. I was busy with another task and told her if I find the tin, her job was to peel the potatoes for dinner. She agreed, and I found it exactly where I had explained it was. She finished making the cake, peeled the potatoes, and I went back to my task. She learned to look more carefully next time.

The inconvenience tax

If our children have forgotten something for school that affects other people or their final grade, and we are available, Denny or I will take it to them. However, there was an inconvenience tax applied. If it took us an hour out of our day, they owe us an hour of their time. Instead of watching TV for an hour, they were required to help with extra jobs and tasks around the house. These tasks were usually the "I'll get around to that" tasks, such as wiping the skirting boards and cleaning the light switches. Often our son would help me with filing, typing or data entry in the office. Children quickly learn to plan, think ahead and take responsibility for their commitments.

A hanky, my lunch and lesson plans

When I was training to be a teacher, I had a teaching practice in my home town. I was able to stay with Mum and Dad for six weeks. It was a wonderful time, being back home in familiar surroundings and back to my roots. Each day before I left for school, my Mum would ask me if I had a handkerchief, my lunch and my lesson plans. I was twenty-one years old and would roll my eyes silently each day. One day she didn't ask, and I forgot my lunch! I was starving when I arrived home as I was too embarrassed to say anything and the school was in the country, a long drive from any shops. I learned a valuable lesson: to listen to my Mum and, most of all, to do my check before I left the house each day. Now, I always stop at the front door and do a mental preview of the day and go through my mental 'checklist' to ensure I have everything I need.

If we as parents constantly remind our children, they do not have to think nor take responsibility. Step back and allow them to learn the consequences. If they forget their lunch, they will not die. If they don't have their raincoat and it starts to rain, they will get wet. They will not melt.

I love this sign from a school:

One of the most frustrating parts of parenting is seeing your child have the same experience over and over again until they learn it. This is how the learning process works. Use some coaching techniques and gentle questioning instead of simply telling children what they need to do. Ask, "What do you need today to make your day successful?" or "Have you got everything you need for today." Again resist the often strong desire to rescue. Your job is to empower.

A time for kindness

There are times it is OK to rescue your child. Maybe it is not rescuing. It is showing kindness and empathy. For example, If you are out on a walk and it gets freezing, and they didn't bring a jacket and are shivering, give them your coat. This is about role modelling kindness rather than rescuing. It is a fine line. Do what is suitable for you and your child. If the behaviour of not taking responsibility in a particular area keeps coming up repeatedly, then the lesson is perhaps not being learned.

> *I've learned so much from my mistakes, I'm thinking of making a few more.*
>
> —Unknown

CHAPTER 4

RUNNING WITH SCISSORS

> *I've learned that no matter how you try to protect your children, they will eventually get hurt, and you will hurt in the process.*
>
> -U<small>NKNOWN</small>

If I have a soapbox, perhaps it is about the importance of allowing children to learn from their mistakes. It is a theme throughout this book. I often find myself noticing others engaging in 'rescue' parenting and stopping children from learning from those mistakes and failures.

I'm convinced it is fear that drives us. Let me explain…

A few years ago, Denny & I, with our two kids, were coming back from an overseas holiday and were disembarking at a very late hour. We were all tired and hungry and still had another flight to catch before making it home. We were travelling with my parents, and they were seated further down the aeroplane. Our young daughter disembarked and, wanting to wait for her grandparents, sat on the floor, around the first corner of the corridor, and in the main foot traffic flow of others leaving the plane. She was tucked in close to the wall.

However, it was not the best place to sit. I overheard Denny telling her to shift as others would stand on her. She refused to move, and he kept on insisting someone would trip or stand on her. While his intentions were great, he failed to understand that she was likely to prove him wrong with that simple statement.

Denny was driven by fear. The fear of her getting hurt, fear of others judging him, fear of being reprimanded by the airport staff, and so on.

On the other hand, she proved him wrong because no-one stood or tripped on her. She stood up once her grandparents appeared and carried on. In her mind, she created a meaning that she might not trust his warnings in the future.

I can recall as a child travelling in the car's back seat on a hot summer's day. I reached my arm outside the window with the window down and the breeze blowing. I strongly remember my Dad cautioning me never to put my arm outside the window while the car was moving. I questioned him as to why it was not allowed to be told if the car rolled with my arm out the window, I might lose my limb. From my Dad's perspective, he knew someone whose car rolled, and they lost an arm and was protecting me.

Even way back then, I silently questioned the validity and likelihood of this ever happening. It was a rule-based on fear and minuscule odds of it ever happening. I was more likely to win the lottery.

Fear v's danger

> *Fear is not real. It is the product of thoughts you create. Danger is very real, but fear is a choice.*
>
> -WILL SMITH

Fear is what often drives us, and when we hold our children back because of our fear, they are less likely to learn for themselves and will not develop the resilience and essential life skills needed in their future. The Merriam-Webster Dictionary describes fear as "an unpleasant and often strong emotion caused by anticipation or awareness of danger." We are wired as humans to protect our young. We often try to protect them from events that may or may not happen. There is, however, a difference between fear and danger. In the modern, busy, in your face world, we live in, the brain has perhaps been confused by the two.

After a lengthy discussion with Educational Psychologist Kathryn Berkett, she shared this: (I have paraphrased our conversation.)

We are born knowing what a primary threat is. Children are born instinctually knowing that snakes and spiders directly threaten them. It makes sense when you think historically, both spiders and snakes could have killed you. There is so much of the brain that has not changed over centuries of evolving – and this is one example. She explained if a child has a fear of mice, this is a learned response. Mice have never been a primary threat to the human species' existence.

I recently explained this at a workshop in Africa, and one of my participants, Maria, shared this example. Her mother was afraid of heights, and as a child, Maria has perfectly happy being up high. One day Maria got too close to the edge of a tall building, and her mother freaked out. Maria explained she is now petrified of heights and breaks into a sweat when up high.

As a parent, be mindful of your fears and separate these from actual danger for your children. It can be easy to influence our children to 'buy in' to our fears or, conversely, learn not to believe you because what you are concerned about never eventuates.

Be aware of your own biases and fears and work towards minimising the transfer of these to your children.

Scrolling the internet for common fears, I came upon a list from listverse.com. Here they stated the ten most common fears which influence human behaviour. They are:

Ten common fears (in descending order)

10. Losing your freedom
9. The unknown
8. Physical pain
7. Disappointment
6. Misery
5. Loneliness
4. Ridicule
3. Rejection
2. Death
1. Failure

Fascinating that failure is the number one fear. Making mistakes and being wrong is how we learn. Remember your child learning to ride a bike? They didn't fall off once and go back to trainer wheels forever. They just kept on going until they could ride. Consider how much attention you gave to each little micro win in the process. You applauded, praised, laughed and encouraged. Now think about them doing their maths homework or writing a card for Grandma. Do you give the same kind of positive attention to the micro wins, the progress and improvements they make?

Essential life skills and dispositions of successful people include taking risks, giving new things a go, creativity and thinking flexibly (more of this is chapter 8). All of these require the possibility of making a mistake and being wrong. It is a feeling and an opportunity children must learn to contend with and master.

> *Fall seven times and stand up eight*
>
> -JAPANESE PROVERB

The philosophy behind this famous proverb is great to explore. In reality, if you fall down seven times, you get up seven times. The eighth time refers to knowing that you are likely to fall or make a mistake again every time you get up. It is part of the learning process.

Experiential learning

When our children were young, they played in the kitchen cupboards while I was cooking. I lost count of how many times I heard other adults say, "Watch your fingers." It was more likely for you to hear me say, "Catch your fingers!" The best way for them to learn is to catch a finger in the door. They are extremely unlikely to do it again. We've all, at some point in our lives, caught our fingers in a cupboard or drawer. It's called being human!

As much as you want to protect your child from hurt and disappointment, you can't.

After New Zealand's first Covid 19 Lockdown in 2020, the courier industry saw unprecedented growth. One of our local owner-operated couriers stopped outside our house and asked our Miss 18 if she would like a job to be a runner. This involved travelling in the courier van's passenger seat and jumping out to leave the parcels at people's doors, leaving the driver (the owner) to concentrate on the next stop and speed up the delivery process. Miss 18 accepted and was instructed to wear black leggings, and she would be picked up the following Tuesday at 10 am. Our daughter was thrilled. It would be her first 'official' job. She purchased new leggings, made lunch, packed snacks and was nervously waiting on our driveway at 9.45 am. Ten o'clock came, ten-fifteen, ten-thirty. She walked into my office (I assumed she had gone), wondering what to do. My mind raced. Did she get the wrong day? The incorrect time? Finally, with some coaxing, she texted the courier. A message came back thirty minutes later to say the boss had found someone else and sorry they thought they had messaged to tell her!

Our daughter was devastated. It broke my heart as she sobbed into my shoulder. Once she was calm, we chatted about the lessons and the need for contracts in writing. I praised her for her willingness to take the job and her organisation skills to be ready for the day.

Sometimes, the lessons are complicated, and these experiences can make your child more resilient and internally strong when taking responsibility and learning the lessons.

Learning the hard way

When our daughter was eight years old, she went to help her Uncle feed the pigs on the farm. They came to an electric fence, and she was advised to keep away and not touch it. After minutes of asking why she was not allowed to touch it (her attempt to understand how it all works) and was advised it would give her an electric shock, her Uncle finally suggested she touch it then. She did. She experienced a slight jolt and will never do it again! Some children do need to learn the hard way!

Saying this, I am not suggesting you allow your child to play with a metal fork near a power socket. We do have a duty to protect them from harm. Of course, they must wear a helmet on their bike, a seatbelt whilst in the car, and we must keep boiling water out of children's reach.

The distinction is to ensure your fears are not transferred to your child. Allow them to learn, make judgements and experiment to find the boundaries.

Learning from others

> *Learn from the mistakes of others. You can't live long enough to make them all yourself.*
>
> -Eleanor Roosevelt

Often, children do not need to learn from their own mistakes and can learn from others' failures.

Our son was five years old and daughter three when I did a national book tour promoting my latest book. We went as a family. Denny drove. They would drop me at the venue each morning and go off and explore the town and pick me up at 12.30 pm. We ate lunch and drove to the next town, checking into a motel or hotel. This pattern continued for two weeks. One afternoon, at a motel in Auckland, our son had left the sliding door open. I asked him to close it. As he did, he caught his finger in the door. There was a great deal of screaming and crying as we ran this first finger under the cold tap. It went black very quickly, and there was nothing broken. Once all was settled down, I noticed the door was again open. This time I asked Miss 3 to please close the door. She looked at her brother, walked to the door, placed her palms on the glass, slid the door closed and announced. "I be careful!"

The phrase 'don't run with scissors' had become synonymous with rebellious or reckless behaviour, like 'living on the edge' or 'playing with fire.'

The next time you hear yourself say, "Don't run with the scissors," stop and reflect on is it an actual danger or a personal fear. Is there a reality to your concern, or is it a result of the thoughts and fears you have created?

Upon researching the phrase, "don't run with scissors", I found that children are more likely to cut their fingers with a pair of scissors (72% of injuries compared to .0008% of children hurt while running with scissors) and are far more likely to be injured from coins, benches and handrails.

CHAPTER 5

CREATING FAMILY TRADITIONS

> *The most treasured heirlooms are the sweet memories of our family that we pass down to our children.*
>
> -U<small>NKNOWN</small>

Parenting is one of those occupations where you are the most amazing at it until you have kids! It often feels like a never-ending and constant search for ideas and techniques to ease the frustration and increase the fun factor.

One of the most tangible ways to build a strong foundation for your children is to create family traditions. Traditions will reinforce your values and create stability (the roots) of safety and strengthen family bonds. They also provide a source of identity for both the children and parents. As a working and travelling Mum, these were also really important. Having a routine, a 'way we do it around here,' made my parenting easier. A bonus is that our children may repeat these in their home and our grandchildren in their families one day, creating a remarkable legacy from your parenting.

As a parent, I feel so fortunate to stand on the shoulders of so many. Over the years, I have met many incredible people who have shared parenting tips, and they have had an enormous impact on my parenting style. Some of these people I still know, and others have been forgotten. My sincere thanks to them for your ideas and tips.

Here are some of our favourite family rituals and traditions.

A month in the front

Our children seem to fight about the smallest of tasks. We constantly heard, "It's not fair! He fed the fish yesterday." "She did the plates on the table 2 days in a row!" or "I never get to…" It seemed endless. Then I learned this concept from my friend, Verity, 'A month in the front.'

Simply allocate a month for each child. We rotated from child one to child two in our house, and the adults shared a month. If it was your month, you could choose the best jobs for a month. It was the small things; preferring to set the plates on the table and not the cutlery, sitting in the car's front seat (when it is free), etc.

When it is the adults month, the children shared the tasks and learned to cooperate, knowing their month was coming. This has become so ingrained into our family, I don't even know whose month it is – but the kids do!

Dinner time

Dinner time is almost a sacred time in our home. It's a chance to be together, share, chat and learn. Too often, this time is sacrificed in busy households, and at times, it has been hard to maintain with sports, cultural activities and the general hecticness of family life. As often as possible, we gather around the table to share a meal.

We have created a ritual of a question of the day. When the children were small, we asked, "What is your favourite part of your day?" As they grew, we added, "What are you grateful for?" and a few years ago, we also added a question from a colleague, Rowie, "What positive difference in the world have you made today?" The dialogue which followed was powerful and often intense. We have also created a Questions At the Dinner Table list, which you can find in Appendix 3.

No technology at the table

Before our children even had personal phones, we made a rule; no phones at the table. Denny and I practised not answering our phones and modelling the behaviour we wanted our children to exhibit. It is often challenging to ignore the urgency of a phone ringing. There is a compulsion to answer. The underlying message we were sending to our children was 'nothing is as important as you are.' This rule was easy to enforce once the children had their phones because we had modelled it. We also maintained a strict regime of the television being off while eating. This meant there were no major external disruptions or distractions, and we could talk and share more freely as a family.

Rites of passage

As the eldest child in my family, I constantly had to wait until my younger sister was old enough to do an activity or receive a privilege. Often, a milestone I had to wait for was given to my sister at the same time. This was something I wanted to avoid in our family. I wanted to create a level of fairness and anticipation.

With more than one child, it is often challenging to recall at what age you gave each child a privilege or special event. Denny and I created a small timeline of when we felt it was appropriate for certain events to occur and particular age. (We often made this up as we went along; however, it was important for the younger child to know when to expect the event.) Of course, your timeline will be very different from ours and should be. Do what is suitable for your family and children.

Age 8: Pocket money – this was their age in dollars (See Pocket money ideas further later in this chapter). We kept this going until they were sixteen, by which time they needed to have their own source of income.

Age 8: (or somewhere in that year when we felt the child was ready and questioning) The birds and the bees talk. The basics were explained with both parents present and with the aid of the book *Where Did I Come From* by Peter Mayle. The book was then theirs to keep.

Age 10: Explained the truth about Santa. While many people disagree, it was a critical moment in both our children's lives when we were upfront and honest and recalled the fun and excitement that the 'story' had given over the years. It was a big relief for our son as he had heard from other children and was grappling with the incongruency of message between his peers and parents.

Age 11: We stopped automatically hosting birthday parties, and the children could choose between a party or $200 in their savings account. (Up until this age, we hosted birthday parties with their age number as guests invited.)

Age 11: Cook a meal a week – yes, the whole thing! The children have always helped in the kitchen and were gifted a cookbook on their eleventh birthday. Macaroni cheese was a staple dish cooked for a while!

Age 12: Set up a social media page together and post together throughout the year while talking about cyber safety. (I believe it is easier to sit with your child and monitor their online behaviour at 12 than 13 when they are naturally pushing for more independence)

Age 13: Given a cell phone for their birthday. (This may need to be earlier for some children) Our daughter bypassed this slightly by saving up to buy her phone at 12!

Age 15/16: At this age, we strongly advised and coached them to get a part-time job. A job helps them learn about time management, gives them work experience, shortens the free time they have to engage in risky behaviours, gives them more independence, builds self-confidence and a sense of responsibility. Once our children had a job, they were also responsible for paying for their phones, haircuts, snack food, personal outings (movies etc.), trains, Ubers and sports fees.

Age 18: The coming of age to adulthood. (Some would argue that it doesn't happen until age 21 or later!) Eighteen is the age in New Zealand when teens can vote, legally drink alcohol and get into night clubs. At this age, we created an 'Adult Child Living At Home Contract.' See Appendix 4. This outlines their roles and responsibilities as a contributing adult within our home and the rent they will pay. The rent is negotiated according to their earning capacity.

Pocket money

There are many ways you can give pocket money to your child. Pick a system that works well for your family. Here are some options:

- Every child gets the same amount each week (this didn't fit into our philosophy of a rite of passage)
- Pay each child their age in money. At eight, they get $8, at 13 $13 etc.
- Link pocket money to tasks that must be completed every week. This would be a fixed amount each week with a pre-arranged list of tasks to be completed.
- Create a pay rate per job or task so your child can earn more if they put in the effort.
- You might create a bonus payment for jobs completed without being asked.

Many years ago, I came across this excellent money box that teaches children about personal finance and wealth. It had four compartments; Give, Live, Save & Wealth – with the latter two compartments screwed shut to avoid spontaneous withdrawals. I'm not sure if these are still available. The same concept can be created with jars or four money boxes.

Our expectations were simple. From your pocket money, $1 must go into the Give slot. This is the tithing money for charity, buskers, donations or put towards our sponsor child in Africa.

When they gifted a goat to our sponsor child for Christmas, the pride on our children's faces was priceless.

A minimum of two dollars must go into both the Save and Wealth sections. The remaining money went into the Live compartment.

Living is for the week to week needs such as treats, two-dollar shop purchases, buying something from the market etc. This is their own money to spend as they see fit, without parent approval. If we were shopping and saw something they wanted, I simply asked if they had enough money in their living account. I quickly discovered when it was up to them to fund the purchase, and they often decided it was not that important!

The savings goes toward a more significant item they wish to purchase. Our son spent two years saving for his iPad while our daughter used this money to buy her first phone. Spending this money must meet with parental approval.

Wealth is money to invest for growth. Both our children have a small share in forestry in NZ. This is all about 'getting into the habit' of being money-wise.

Now they are older, and they have a similar set up with bank accounts. A percentage of their wages goes into their wealth account, which will eventually be part of a house deposit or something that will grow their money. This money is not for buying a car. A car is a liability rather than an investment as the purchase price will only go down, unlike a house when over time, the purchase price goes up.

Now they are independently earning, it was a straight forward decision to live on seventy percent of their wage and allocate the rest.

Monthly family day

Each month we schedule a family day, usually during the weekend. Each person was allocated a month aligned with the 'a month in the front' earlier in this chapter. It was that person's task to choose the activity, research it and plan the day. The only rule was you cannot do what was done last month or what you designed the previous time. There was an available budget of $50 for the day, including any food purchases. It was becoming harder and harder to do something with a family of 4 for under $50, and we all become pretty creative in the process! The children watched the specials and deals closely and often planned a picnic, walk or drive, which did not cost. The older the children became, the more sport they seem to be involved in, so this tradition has become more of a bi-monthly occurrence. We'd often make a sports game a family time with a small picnic or walk on the beach afterwards.

National Wagging Day

Inspired by the Pumpkin Patch clothing retailer founder, Sally Synott, we now have an annual National Wagging Day. On a weekday, all of us wag (or skip) school or work. Sometimes we'd go to the zoo, stay in bed and watch movies all day in our PJ's, go for a picnic, a walk or hang out and play cards and board games together. Usually, Denny and I pre-scheduled this day, so it didn't clash with a school event or our work. My favourite part of the day was when I told the kids they couldn't go to school today. There is always an outcry, "I want to go to school!" and I tell them they can't. Of course, this was the opposite of most days when they protested they didn't want to go to school. This day usually happened in the third term when we were tired and sick of the cold winters days.

Friday pizza night

This tradition came out of a time of financial tension and the fact that we couldn't buy takeaways for a few months. As a family, we would all gather in the kitchen. Denny would cut up the leftover cold potatoes from previous nights and cook them into chips. I would make pizza dough by hand, and the children would cut up the pizza toppings and make their pizzas. It was a great time of fun and laughter and jostling for space at the bench to cook. This custom has been so ingrained that even when we can buy takeaways, we still make homemade pizza. Friends even love joining us for Pizza night and often bring their favourite toppings.

As with building any ritual or tradition, the key to these ideas' success is our consistency to uphold and execute the ideas. They have become the "this is how we do it around here" customs. I genuinely believe it has created more stability and certainty in our home and increased our closeness and fun factor as a family.

Reading through these ideas might have felt overwhelming. We grew these over time. Start with one and do it for 2-3 months and then add another. Do what is suitable for your family.

Most importantly, create your own traditions and rituals.

We are certainly not perfect at any of this, and we are still searching for more ideas and continue to bring new techniques to our parenting toolbox. It's not too late to start.

> *Family traditions reveal what you value enough to repeat, and if done with love, build warm, happy associations.*
>
> -Daniel Willingham

CHAPTER 6

SCHOOL HOLIDAY CHALLENGES

> *In school, children complain they need a holiday. In the holidays, they complain it's boring and wanna to go back to school.*
>
> -U<small>NKNOWN</small>

There tend to be two camps of parents when it comes to school holidays. You either dread or love the thought of having your children at home for two weeks. I believe holidays are a chance for children to relax and kick back, and for families to connect and make memories. School holidays were also a time to relax some of the expectations and boundaries that pertained to school. For example, bedtimes were extended slightly, and high sugar cereals were allowed.

Over the years, I have created special family challenges in the school holidays, making memories, fun, laughter, bonding, and learning. We use the word challenge with our children as all four of us have a keen competitive spirit. You might wish to soften the experience with other words. And best of all it has cost us nothing, except 30-60 minutes each day, oh and ice cream!

Here are some of our favourites.

The no technology challenge

Three days, yes you read that correctly, three whole days with no technology: no phones, no computers, no TV! According to my children, I'm such a mean Mum, and they secretly love it. Out came the board games, the make and do, their bikes, books etc. and best of all, they develop the essential life skill of creativity.

While children are hooked on screens, the brain's creativity muscle does not get a workout, as images and ideas are supplied. Having nothing to do and being bored is an ideal time for the brain to think, create and imagine.

> *I think it is necessary to let kids get bored once in a while- that's how they learn to be creative.*
>
> -KIM RAVER

It is essential to give your child time to be bored. Being bored forces a child to be creative and 'find' something to do. It helps them learn to use their initiative and develop grit and boost their self-esteem. They can try new things, take risks, test limits and develop problem-solving skills.

Create a space for the No Tech Challenge. Start by warning your children which days it will be, keep to your word and leave them to their 'devices', pun intended! If they say they 'won't let you' take their devices, remove the phones, remotes and chargers while they are asleep. This way, they wake up fresh, with no access to technology.

Resist filling in the time for them. Ignore the constant pleas for the tech back. They will attempt to drive you crazy and test your resolve.

The first time you do this, day one will be the hardest! After that, they resign themselves to the fact that they can push and argue or get on with life. One of my children would do a spectacular performance in an attempt to change my mind. I would simply smile and tell them that, channelled in the right way, their persistence will be a great asset in the future.

You can do this challenge every holiday! We did. Let the fun begin!

> *To be in your child's memories tomorrow, you have to be in their lives today.*
>
> -BARBARA JOHNSON

The Knucklebones (Jacks) challenge

I didn't play knucklebones as a child, so we were all starting on a reasonably even playing field – or so I thought. Each night after dinner, the four of us, Mum, Dad and two kids, sat on the floor and learned the game. We googled the rules and levels, and off we went. The competition started getting fierce when we all realised that Dad (who have never played in his life before) had bigger hands and could catch all five knucklebones on the back of his hand and therefore skipped up the levels very quickly. The children would 'secretly' practice during the day in a bid to beat their Dad. The last day of the holidays was the crowning of the Champion of Champions – we played until there was a clear winner.

The gratitude challenge

A gratitude challenge was relatively simple yet caused a great deal of conversation and thinking over the two weeks. I attached a huge piece of blank chart paper to the kitchen wall. Each day, usually after dinner, we would write three things we were grateful for that day. During those two weeks, every person who visited us also added their gratitudes to the chart. After two weeks, we talked about how grateful we are as a family and its impact on our lives. This challenge has been repeated many times over the years, especially in the cold winter months. See chapter 11 for more about gratitude.

The Bucket List challenge

One of our most involved holiday tasks was to create a book of notes and a poster of our bucket list. Inspired by Travis Bell, the Bucket List Guy*, we went through each day looking at one aspect of our future and what we would like to be, do or have. The categories were:

M = Meet a personal hero
Y = Your proud achievements
B = Buy that something special
U = Ultimate Challenge
C = Conquer a fear
K = Kind Acts of Others
E = Express Yourself
T = Travel Adventures
L = Leave a legacy
I = Idiotic Stuff
S = Satisfy a Curiosity
T = Take Lessons

We brainstormed one letter/category in a random order each night and created a poster with photos, pictures, and words at the end of two weeks. These are still displayed in our kitchen today.

* You can find more about Travis Bell and his Bucket List process at www.thebucketlistguy.com. I have also blogged about our two weeks, and you can find the information here: www.karentuiboyes.com/2014/10/our-family-bucket-lists-goal-setting-for-the-future/

Here are our charts:

The clean your room/ice cream challenge

I love this one. Each holiday, and occasionally mid-term, I offer the ice cream challenge. Simply put, clean your room, to my standard, in less than an hour, and I'll buy you an ice cream! This included dusting, vacuuming and clearing out the clutter. When they were younger, I would do it with them, teaching and showing them how to tidy their room. Once to my standard, I took photos and displayed them inside their wardrobe door for future reference.

It is simple, fun and the rooms get tidy. While they sometimes moaned and complained throughout (I would just ignore it), they would play their favourite music (loud), and I constantly gave the countdown – "40 minutes to go", 20 minutes to go", "5 minutes to go." It is fun and effective, and of course, no-one wants to miss out on the ice cream, so they both participated fully. Naturally, if only one child completes the challenge, only one goes out for ice cream.

Other family challenges included the board game challenge, the ukulele challenge and the step challenge! Maybe I will even add in a dance challenge at some stage. Even now they are young adults, I'm making them up as I go along, especially while they are both still living at home!

> *Kid's don't need another friend. What they need is a parent to be a parent.*
>
> —Judge Judy

CHAPTER 7

BOUNDARIES, EXPECTATIONS & REWARDS

> *My goal as a parent is to prepare you for the future – not make you like me.*
>
> -AMY CHUA

Holding appropriate rules and boundaries is perhaps a key responsibility of parents. As the late Celia Lashlie, author and social justice advocate used to say, "Clear boundaries need to be set, but a [child] needs to feel free."

You are not your child's friend; you are their parent. Responsible for their physical and emotional well-being, keeping them safe and helping them navigate and problem-solve the challenges of their lives. Responsible for teaching them right and wrong.

Many times this requires tough love, saying no and also trusting.

It is like a game of netball. There are positions and boundaries. Certain players can only play in specific areas of the court, and if a player or the ball goes outside those pre-determined boundaries, the whistle goes, and play is paused. The umpire explains why the stoppage, the infringement, and the game is resumed. Within limits, players are free to move and play the game.

Set your boundaries and leave your child free to roam within these. When they cross a boundary, let them know. If and when appropriate, give a pre-determined consequence and teach the desired behaviour.

We have an agreement in our home that everyone must say hello when you get home (even if it is 3 am) and goodbye before you leave. For me, this is simple politeness. Once, our daughter left with her friends without saying goodbye. When I realised they had all gone, I called her on her phone, let her know she had crossed one of my boundaries. She was most apologetic, and it has never happened again. Her friends also always come and say hi and let me know when leaving. This might seem like an insignificant rule and example, however, if I had let it slide, it opens the way for other rules to be broken.

When you are tired and busy, sometimes it just seems easier to pick up their toys, tidy up their bedroom or put their dirty dishes away. Resist. The effort you muster to ask them to fulfil their duty will be worth it in the long term. Even with all their complaining and moaning, it is still worth holding the boundaries.

Denny and I see the fruits of our efforts as our children get older. Recently we had two teens staying with us for nearly a year. It was great to hear Miss 18 grumble and gripe about them leaving shoes on the floor and not stacking the dishwasher. I would smile and nod in affirmation of the journey she has been on and her understanding of the frustration that this causes.

Boundaries create security and safety in a home. It's the 'this is the way we do it around here.' Consistency is the key. When the rules constantly change or are not reinforced, children are unsure how far they can go or push. Most children will push to find the boundaries and test to see how firm they are.

Decide on your rules and display them. Some of our family rules are displayed at the entrance to our home.

Punishment versus discipline

Last year, I enjoyed interviewing parenting expert Dr Justin Coulson for my Parenting for Resilience, Confidence & Independence Online Summit. A significant distinction I learned from him was the difference between punishment and discipline.

Just in explained that punishment is designed to hurt your child, and discipline helps. Hurting your child by asserting your higher authority and power over them teaches the child that adults don't care, you can get whatever you want by asserting your power and that it's OK to push smaller people around. Punishment includes smacking, time out, withdrawal of privileges etc. Usually, a punishment intends to have a child reflect on how their behaviour has impacted others; however, what they think about is themself. This leads to becoming more selfish. Relationships are also damaged when punishment is dished out.

The meaning of discipline is to teach, guide or instruct. This means working with your child to ensure they learn and grow. Justin promotes the 3 E's and a C!

- Explain what the expectation was and why what they did wrong, in a calm and kind tone.
- Explore what is going on for your child and their thinking and motivations behind their behaviour. Ensure everyone is feeling understood.

- Empower by asking your child for a solution or a way forward. Ultimately, you want the child to be able to solve their challenges.
- Consequences need to be enacted. If they have broken something, they need to fix it. If they have hurt someone, they must apologise and so on.

Pick your battles

> *If parenting came with a GPS, it would most likely say recalculating.*
>
> -Unknown

Family Therapist Dr Margot Brown promotes the 72-hour rule:

"If it won't matter after 72 hours, it never did. If you don't feel the need to react after 72 hours, don't at all." This is an excellent rule of thumb to live by.

Stop worrying about their bedrooms and pick your battles. Decide what you can control, can't control and want to control.

Whilst some might disagree, I do not allow our children to swear or use curse words in our home. They can (and do) swear outside our house. I'm OK with this as I know they have the self-control to manage their words (and behaviour) in different settings.

Take time out, alone, with your significant other or with a trusted friend and consider what you want more of, less of, what you want to stop doing and start doing.

Pushing the boundaries

Children are great at changing our minds and stretching the boundaries further. One of our agreements was the children could have free access to technology from when they arrived home from school until 9 pm when they were expected to be in their rooms. We also had a rule of no technology allowed in the bedrooms. One night at 8.55 pm, Mr 14 came to me and, in a panic, told me he had just remembered he had a huge assignment due the next day and needed to use the computer. I looked at my watch and informed him he had 5 minutes. He said that that was not enough time and asked for longer. I said no. His little sister, overhearing this, called out, "Well, you shouldn't have been on the Xbox all night, should you!" Out of the mouths of babes! There was the start of a great lesson to be learned! When faced with this dilemma, Mr 14 tried to change my mind. This had three clear phases:

Phase 1: Beg and bargain

"I'll do anything if you just let me have the computer. I'll wash your car, do the dishes for a week, paint the house!" As tempting as it was, I held the boundary tight and advised him he had three and a half minutes left.

Phase 2: Insult and guilt (Always performed at top volume.)

"You are the worst mother in the world! Every other mother would let their kid have the computer. I hate you!" As hurtful as this was, I knew he didn't mean it and held tight to the household rule.

Phase 3: Waterworks

Tears welled up in his eyes and rolled down his cheeks as he sobbed, "You jjjust don't undddderstttand. It's a rrrreally impppportant aaaassignment, and I have to ggget it dddone." Obviously, it was so important he left it to the last minute! And of course, when you are a 14-year-old boy and cry in front of your mother, it must be dire. I informed him he had thirty more seconds.

He turned to me and said, in a calm, rational voice - how do they go from begging, screaming and crying to a quiet tone in such a short time – asked if I would wake him at 6 am so he could do the assignment in the morning.

Our son learned a few lessons on that night. To start with, he realised I was serious about the rule of no-tech after 9 pm. Next, he saw the value of better time management. Lastly, he discovered he was far more productive and focused on working in the early morning.

If I had 'given in' or been lenient by stretching the rule a little, he would not have learned this essential life lesson and might have pushed that boundary more often.

What will other people think?

> *Comparison is the thief of Joy.*
>
> -Theodore Roosevelt

It is easy to look at the social media feeds, and others' Pinterest lives and wish your life was more like theirs. Stop it! They are only showing what they want you to see. Trying to be like everyone else is exhausting and unrealistic.

Parenting Power Speaker, Lisa O'Neil suggests what happens in your home is normal for your family. For example, it is routine for our family to eat dinner at the table together every night, and my children find it unusual that their friends eat in their rooms or in front of the TV. It was natural for our children to have free access to technology from after school until 9 pm on school nights and not have parents nag about getting their homework done. We considered homework their responsibility, not ours, and we're always available to help and assist. They were always surprised when friends had strict times for technology and only after completing two hours of homework.

It doesn't matter if you agree or disagree with our rules; they are our rules.

It's your family, do it your way. What other people think is none of your business!

I'll trust you until I can't

> With freedom comes responsibility. If you want to experience more freedom in life, you must take more responsibilities for your choices.
>
> -UNKNOWN

I have always told my children I love them unconditionally. I will love them when they are compliant, pushing my limits, with passing or failing grades. I will love them if they are in prison. This does not mean I will rescue them from prison! However, I will hold the space to love who they are and learn the lessons required. Our son has seriously tested me at times!

As the children became older and more independent, and I slowly let go of the control, I told them, "I will trust you until I can't." When they said they were going out to the park to play, I trusted this. As they got older, when going out to a party, I trusted them when they said they wouldn't drink, even though I knew their friends were. Neither child has disappointed us in this regard. They have even been the only person at a party not drinking because they were underage. (One of those proud parent moments!)

The secret code

It's probably a great time to mention we had a 'secret code' with our children when they went out to parties. We would either ring or text them at an earlyish time, maybe 10 pm, and Ask, "Do you have sports practice tomorrow?" If the reply was 'no', we knew they were safe and happy. If the response was 'yes', we knew they were either feeling unsafe or were not enjoying themselves, and we would go and pick them up. This was a way to save face in front of their friends and have an out if they needed it.

Holding court

Parenting can feel such a heavy burden at times that Denny and I decided to enjoy the yukky stuff as much as we could. We developed a court system for when our kids had stepped over the line.

I recall Mr 11 sitting at the table's head, with Denny and me on either side, holding court. Our son had overstepped a boundary and was summoned to appear in court. Neither Denny nor I have been to court nor have any legal training. We have simply watched too many TV dramas, and we made it up as we went along.

With a straight face, Denny declared, "This court is in session."

We then proceeded to state the charge and ask how he pleaded. (The first time our daughter appeared in our court, she burst into tears and said, 'I have never been to court before!")

After the 'proceedings', we declared that the court would be adjourned, and their verdict would deliver in three days. The consequence is not delivered on the same day in a real court. We secretly loved holding court. It was fun (for us) and a profound way to keep our children accountable for their actions.

We would ask what their consequences or sentence might be in subsequent court sessions. This proved fascinating as they would often choose something far more severe than we would!

Rewards

> *The highest reward for a person's toil is not what they get for it, but what they become by it.*
>
> -JOHN RUSKIN

The majority of children love receiving awards. When a child is motivated through an extrinsic experience, they will want to repeat the experience over and over again. Once recognised for an achievement, it is likely to increase their efforts in that area. The main reason to reward your child is to reinforce and encourage behaviour or habit you wish them to continue.

Dr Eric Jensen, a world-renowned brain researcher, suggests for rewards to be successful, they must have two elements; be predictable and have market value.

Predictability means children need to know how the system works. A surprise or random reward does not have the effect of reinforcing positive behaviour, so the desired action is unlikely to be repeated. Let your child know when they do a particular task, achieve a specific goal or behave in a certain way what the reward will be.

The second part of effective rewards is market value. Have you ever despaired when your child brings home a crumbled certificate? It is likely to mean the certificate has no market value for that student. Conversely, some students take pride in certificates and display these at home.

Depending on the child's age, stickers, stamps, and stars may have value, and for others, these artefacts have no value. These children might work harder for free time, a treat from the mall or extra time doing what they love. It will differ for each child.

Idealistically, the goal is to remove the external rewards and have your child do the right things because of the internal benefits. External rewards will often be a motivator at some level. Would you go to work each day if you didn't get paid? Even if you love your work, money is a driving factor to feed your family and keep a roof over their head.

CHAPTER 8

SETTING YOUR KIDS UP FOR SUCCESS

There is no such thing as a perfect parent. So be a real one.

-SUE ATKINS

There are so many tiny elements that help set our children up for success. We can't get it right all the time, nor should we.

Each generation takes and learns the best from the previous generation and gets smarter. Now, I know that when you look at your child and their generation, some days this seems a big stretch. If you need convincing, explore MENSA, the largest and oldest high IQ society in the world. You will find that they increase the test's complexity every ten years to gain entry into the echelon. It is often discussed that if Einstein were alive today, he would be in the lower ranks of intelligence. It is called the

Flynn Effect. For each generation, the IQ test scores increase by ten points.

This does not mean you can leave success up to chance. Some key concepts will help your children succeed long term.

Give them something for the counsellor!

I'm 'that' parent who knew I couldn't and wouldn't get 'it' right all the time. Right from naming our children, we discussed the pros and cons of different name choices. We named both our children three years before they were conceived. Hamish was named because of my Denny's Scottish heritage and Sasha from my favourite childhood storybook, *The Silver Seagull* by Pixie Gann, published in 1949. (The book had been my mothers and was old, musty and even had Silverfish within the pages!) It was the middle names that took a while.

We honoured my Maori ancestry and two of my favourite things: rainbows and sunshine. Our children's names are Hamish Niwa (short for āniwaniwa, meaning rainbow) and Sasha Rahana (rā for sun and hana meaning to shine.) Denny and I

often joke that we have our rainbows and sunshine and you have to give kids something to talk to their counsellor about!

My point is not to take yourself so seriously. Do the best you can, and as Kari Sutton in her book *Raising A Mentally Fit Generation* says, Some days will be better than others and "Good enough is really good enough." As Maya Angelou said, "Do the best you can until you know better. Then when you know better, do better."

Ditch self-esteem

Most people reading this book will have grown up in the self-esteem era. In the 1980s, psychologists showed that high self-esteem equated to high grades at school and students with lower self-esteem tended to struggle in school. These same psychologists started a movement to raise self-esteem because they believed that virtually all the world's problems traced back to low self-esteem. So began the participation ribbons, everyone gets a prize (think of the childhood party game pass the parcel) and lavish praise of insignificant achievements.

The flaw in this movement was two-fold. Firstly, self-esteem comes from within, not from what others tell or give you. Being given a ribbon for just entering fosters no real internal sense of satisfaction or confidence. Secondly, self-esteem comes from putting in the effort; trying, iterating, failing, trying again and succeeding.

Our school system reflects these flaws strongly. Children were (and still are in many places) told to go to school and learn – because 'learning is fun'. Learning is complex, messy, challenging, uncomfortable, and something you have to work at. If children believe it should be fun, and it's not, then why even bother. I spend much of my time in schools explaining, "Everything is hard before it is easy" and "The struggle makes you strong."

Furthermore, most students believe the way to succeed at school is to be intelligent, smart and clever. The reality is far from this – to succeed in school (pass the tests and exams), you need to know techniques and strategies for learning, memory recall, test-taking and how your brain works.

> *Success is a lousy teacher. It seduces smart people into thinking they can't lose.*
>
> -BILL GATES

While the self-esteem research initially showed those with higher self-esteem received higher grades in school, subsequent research now indicates it is the other way around. Success and receiving good grades in school raises your self-esteem. The challenge for many is they don't know what they did or how they achieved success in school – it just happened 'by magic.' (There's another book right there!)

Focus on self-control

> *Trophies should go to the winners. Self-esteem does not lead to success in life. Self-discipline and self-control do.*
>
> -ROY BAUMEISTER

Researchers and psychologists now suggest that having self-control is a better precursor of success. This starts at a young age. The famous marshmallow experiment conducted by Stanford University professor and psychologist Walter Mischel in 1972 studied delaying gratification. Children, aged between three and six, were taken into a room and shown one marshmallow on a plate. The children were told that if they waited while the researcher left the room for about 15 minutes, they could have two marshmallows. If they ate the marshmallow, there were no more. The study attributed the ability to wait to delay gratification to higher education and life achievements. In New Zealand, the Dunedin Multidisciplinary Health and Development Research Study, from 1972 to current day, also reflects these findings.

The key to success for the children who waited was to divert their attention elsewhere. Continually staring or looking at the marshmallow meant that at any moment, they were more likely to have a lapse of willpower, and the marshmallow was gone. Those who could divert their attention to another task or focus were more likely to receive the second marshmallow.

The same is true for me. When I crave the chocolate, my willpower is low if I see it in the fridge, and I eat it. If, however, I can distract myself for ten or more minutes, I get absorbed in another task, and the craving goes away, and I forget! (No, I don't get twice as much for waiting; my reward is a healthier, stronger body.*) I feel better about myself, and my self-esteem, self-worth, self-love quotient goes up!

Lessons from Brazil

It is usual for children to be impulsive. At a school in Sao Paulo, Brazil, where I mentored and coached the teachers, Milena, taught three-year-olds to wait and manage themselves.

Firstly she wrapped small gifts for each child. On day one, the gifts were placed in front of each child, and they were asked to wait thirty seconds before opening the gift. This was repeated on day two and three, with wait times extended to sixty and ninety seconds. As you can imagine, this was very challenging for the children. They then discussed strategies for waiting and ways to make it easier. Three simple techniques emerged. 1. Count to ten in your head, 2. Focus on your breath as you breathe in and out, and 3. Drum your fingers on the desk while you wait.

These techniques and explicit teaching were a pre-curser to students learning to take turns, share and sit still in class.

---

* There is nothing wrong with eating chocolate or having a treat now and then. If you are reaching for the chocolate, wine, coffee etc., to escape or block a feeling in an attempt to numb an unconformable emotion or situation, then perhaps you want to look at your motivations and check your actions are aligned with your personal goals.

Fixed & Growth Mindset

> *Talent isn't passed down by genes. It's passed down by mindset.*
>
> —CAROL DWECK

Carol Dweck, Stanford University psychologist, speaks and writes about mindset pertaining to success and achievement. She advocates two types: a fixed mindset and a growth mindset.

People with a fixed mindset believe their intelligence or talents are fixed, and success happens, or it doesn't, depending on their intelligence. People with a growth mindset believe they can develop their essential qualities with effort, focus, training, coaching and hard work.

This table outlines some of the key differences.

A FIXED Mindset Person...	A GROWTH Mindset Person...
Believes intelligence is something you are born with	Believes intelligence comes from hard work and can always improve
Tends to give up easily when faced with a challenge	Embraces challenges as an opportunity to grow
Sees effort as unnecessary and something you do if you are not good enough	Sees effort as essential and as a path to mastery
May take offence to feedback and often takes it personally	Uses feedback as something to learn from and to improve
Blames others and gets discouraged with setbacks	Uses setbacks as an opportunity to work harder next time

Developing a growth mindset is essential for success. A growth mindset involves people developing a love of learning and some resilience. Carol suggests instilling a growth mindset creates motivation and productivity in business, education and sports. She says it also enhances relationships.

Praising repeatable behaviours

> *Praising children's intelligence harms their motivation, and it harms their performance.*
>
> -Carol Dweck

A key to praising your child is to focus on repeatable behaviours rather than intelligence. Praise their effort, concentration, strategies and give specific feedback. Comments such as "Your persistence paid off in completing your homework today" is far more effective than "good job." The pivotal element is to praise repeatable behaviours. Just telling a child, they are a 'good boy/girl' or 'amazing' is not a repeatable behaviour as they often do not know what they did to be 'good' or 'amazing.' Instead, use phrases such as: "Taking the time to go back and check your work has produced a great result." "Wow, you stopped to think about your challenge and have implemented changes to ensure a successful outcome." "Outstanding effort in focusing on the cleaning of your room today."

Notice and reflect on the praise you often hear yourself giving. Is it the effort or final result that you are acknowledging?

I'm going to my room!

Let's face it, parenting is hard at times, and we 'lose it.' I have yelled – loudly and forcefully at my kids at stressful times. I understand I am in control of my emotions. Jodi Richardson, the co-author of *Anxious Kids: How children can turn their anxiety into resilience*, and guest on my Spectrum TV show, explains there are no good or bad emotions – just helpful and unhelpful behaviours. My stress is mine to deal with and not my children's. When I lose that control, rather than letting the guilt override me, I apologise to the child concerned and journal about what was triggering me (it is usually nothing to do with my kids) and how I might respond next time.

One of my favourite responses when our kids were a handful; arguing, not sharing, telling tales over and over etc., and I felt I couldn't cope anymore, was to say, "That's it! I'm going to my room!" I found timeout for me was far more effective than timeout for the kids! They simply sorted out whatever the problem was while I was rocking in my room! Our kids are still the same. They get on so much better when Denny and I are not present. They talk, work together, share, are respectful of each other. It is amazing.

Getting unstuck

> *If plan A doesn't work, there are 25 more letters in the alphabet!*

When your child finds themselves stuck and unsure what to do, teach them how to persist, try again and keep going.

Through their ground-breaking and decades-long research on how humans successfully face challenges, Professor Art Costa and Dr Bena Kallick have identified the 16 Habits of Mind. These are the behaviours of intelligent people and what they do when they are stuck when the answer is not immediately apparent or they are not sure how to move from difficult or challenging situations.

A summary of the 16 Habits of Mind is below. As you read through the list, consider which dispositions or Habits you and your children would benefit from learning.

1. Persisting: *Stick to it!* Persevering in task through to completion; remaining focused. Looking for ways to reach your goal when stuck. Not giving up.

2. Managing Impulsivity: *Take your time!* Thinking before acting; remaining calm, thoughtful and deliberative.

3. Listening with Understanding and Empathy: *Understand others!* Devoting mental energy to another person's thoughts and ideas; Making an effort to perceive another's point of view and emotions.

4. Thinking Flexibly: *Look at it another way!* Being able to change perspectives, generating alternatives, considering options.

5. Thinking about Thinking (Metacognition): *Know your knowing!* Being aware of your own thoughts, strategies, feelings and actions and their effects on others.

6. Striving for Accuracy: *Check it again!* Always doing your best. Setting high standards. Checking and finding ways to improve constantly.

7. Questioning and Posing Problems: *How do you know?* Having a questioning attitude; knowing what data is needed & developing questioning strategies to produce those data. Finding problems to solve.

8. Applying Past Knowledge to New Situations: *Use what you learn!* Accessing prior knowledge; transferring knowledge beyond the situation in which it was learned

9. Thinking and Communicating with Clarity and Precision: *Be clear!* Striving for accurate communication in both written and oral form; avoiding over-generalisations, distortions, deletions and exaggerations.

10. Gathering Data through All Senses: *Use your natural pathways!* Paying attention to the world around you. Gathering data through all the senses; taste, touch, smell, hearing and sight.

11. Creating, Imagining, Innovating: *Try a different way!* Generating new and novel ideas, fluency, originality

12. Responding with Wonderment and Awe: *Have fun figuring it out!* Finding the world awesome, mysterious and being intrigued with phenomena and beauty.

13. Taking Responsible Risks: *Venture out!* Being adventuresome; living on the edge of one's competence. Try new things constantly.

14. Finding Humour: *Laugh a little!* Finding the whimsical, incongruous and unexpected. Being able to laugh at one's self.

15. Thinking Interdependently: *Work together!* Being able to work in and learn from others in reciprocal situations. Teamwork.

16. Remaining Open to Continuous Learning: *Learn from experiences!* Having humility and pride when admitting we don't know; resisting complacency.

It is important to note that no-one ever masters these sixteen Habits of Mind. It is the constant striving to get better at the Habits and as the sixteenth habit outlines, remaining open to continuous learning, which allows us to progress and improve.

For more information, please go to www.habitsofmindinstitute.org

> *Encourage and support your kids because children are apt to live up to what you believe of them.*
>
> —Lady Bird Johnson

> *The issue is that self-care does not equate to how much you accomplish in a day, it has to do with how you feel about yourself, your life, and how you are navigating through your day to day.*
>
> —Aman Litt

CHAPTER 9

SELF-CARE AND FINDING YOU

> ❝ *Self-care is giving the world the best of you, instead of what's left of you.* ❞
>
> -Katie Reed

Losing who you are is one of the worst feelings. Both Denny and I have done this. For me, it was in the early years when the children were young, and Denny, in the years he was a full-time Dad.

Parenting can be all-consuming and losing yourself in the process can be a very dark place. The good news if you are there right now or heading in that direction, you can turn it around. We did.

Order of importance

For some, this may feel uncomfortable to read. I am extremely clear on the order of importance in my life. It is me first, my husband second, the children third, and my work forth.

Me first. If and when my needs are taken care of – it is so much easier to be a wife, lover, Mum, business owner, friend etc. This is not about being entitled, it is about ensuring I have the energy and fuel I need to give to others. You don't drive your car with an empty petrol tank, and we can't give from nothing for very long.

Your glass

Is the glass half-full or half-empty? This is such an age-old question, and I'd like to offer two more perspectives.

Firstly, be thankful you have a glass. From a parenting lens, when my children and driving me up the wall, it serves me well to remember how lucky I am to have children. (Even when I would sell them in a heartbeat or pay someone to have them! Joking!) After over fifteen years of trying everything and experiencing many heartbreaks, my sister remains childless. Having children is a privilege denied to many.

Secondly, it's not a question of half-full or empty, your cup needs to be overflowing. Filling your cup is about doing the activities that fill you with joy, fill your soul with contentment and make you feel alive. Once your cup is full, keep going and let it overflow.

It is the overflow we give to our partner, children, friends and work. I'm not saying I'm not interested in my husband's and children's lives. I'm their number one fan! I'm suggesting you take time each day to do something small (or big) for yourself so you more energy for them.

Consider what you want for your children. Do you want them to be sacrificing their happiness, joy and or wellbeing for others? Or would you rather they are happy, healthy and strong and give to others? I'm guessing it is the latter. You are the role model for this! This isn't about being disrespectful of other's needs, it is simply ensuring you keep refilling your cup to have the vitality to give and be of service.

The burnt chop syndrome

I first heard this concept from the amazing Parenting Power speaker, Lisa O'Neil. Lisa described the burnt chop syndrome at the Parenting For Resilience, Confidence & Independence Online Summit. It is a wonderful metaphor for self-care and filling your cup. Have you ever cooked dinner and there is one chop that is burnt? Whose plate do you dish it on to? Usually your own. We often give our loved ones the best bits and sacrifice ourselves to having the burnt chop as this saves all the moaning, groaning, and drama.

Lisa's mantra is if you did all the work, you get the best part. She tells the story of how when dishing up the evening meal she has prepared, she lays all the plates out and thinks, which child do

I not like as much today and gives them the burnt chop. (There are days we like our children less!) She gives herself the best one. When the children notice, she simply explains she did the work and gets the best one. Quickly the children realise if they do the work, they can have the best one!

> *I make a point to practice self-care. I make an appointment with myself.*
>
> -MANISHA SINGAL MD

Looking after you

Sometimes it may feel like there is no time in the day to look after your own needs. If you are using time as an excuse, it is a clear sign that you are not prioritising your self-care. Self-care does not mean you have to spend hours doing something for yourself. Start with doing something for five minutes every day, then extend it to ten, fifteen minutes. Even if you have to get up slightly earlier or go to bed a little later, you will find that the benefits outweigh the perceived negatives over time. The key is to find something to fill your cup every day.

In their book, Kim Morrison & Fleur Whelligan, *Like Chocolate for Women*, describe a simple two-minute whole body self-massage using aromatherapy oils after a shower. Or maybe after dropping the kids off at school, you take a five-minute walk in the forest or along a river to breathe in nature. Perhaps you sit in the sun for fifteen minutes with a great book after you have completed some tasks. Do some crafting. Whatever fills you up and refreshes and recharges you.

> *Children are great imitators. Give them something great to imitate.*
>
> *-UNKNOWN*

When your needs are met, it is so much easier to be a loving person to your partner or significant other. When I look after myself, I have an extra spring in my step and more energy for those I love. Denny is my second priority in my life as he is my co-parent, my co-pilot and we are doing this parenting gig together. Some days it's super hard as a parent, and I want him there to support and take over if required.

One day the children will be gone, and it will be just the two of us. Our relationship deserves to be important. It is also excellent role modelling for our children in how to have and maintain a loving relationship. This doesn't mean Denny and I don't fight or disagree. We do. Then we work through whatever is going on and support each other.

We have seen counsellors, parenting experts and psychologists together over the years. On occasion, we have asked friends to help. Having an external person to give perspective has been invaluable. We have both have had (and will likely continue) to confront some deep emotions, and being there for each other has strengthened our relationship.

It is a give and take. If he wants an afternoon to play golf, I encourage him to go. If I want a weekend with a girlfriend, he gives me his blessing. It has not always been like this, and we are both a work in progress.

We have couch night at least once a week. This is our time to snuggle and watch our favourite TV show together. If our kids come to chat with us or can't find something during this time, we tell them they can wait until the show is over. It's our time. Now our children are older, we prioritise a weekend away together every 6-8 weeks. (I save fifty dollars a week into a 'couples time' bank account for this.) Often we don't go far. We book an Airbnb house a 1-2 hour drive from our home and spend the weekend enjoying one another's company. We read, play cards, snuggle, walk on the beach – it doesn't matter what we do, it is just our time together. Do what works for you.

> *Loving others is easy when you love and accept yourself.*
>
> -LOUISE HAY

I don't know how to express how much I love my children and how much more I love them when fulfilled in myself and my relationship. It is something you just need to experience. That means putting in the work and making yourself a priority. Our children know we will drop everything for them if they are in trouble. They know we are available to chat and give guidance if they want it. As they let go of the apron strings and as we gradually give them more responsibility for independence, I know my relationship with myself and Denny is a solid foundation from which they springboard from.

Your work does not define you

As parents, we wear many hats, and none of these hats or roles individually define us. I love my work and the difference I get to make in the world and intend to still be of service to the world to the end of my days. (I'll be the oldest professional speaker in the world at 120 years of age!) Yet my work is not what defines who I am.

Designing who you want to be

> *You have the power to change the beliefs about yourself. Your identity is not set in stone. You have choice in every moment.*
>
> -JAMES CLEAR

If you are lost and unsure who you are, there is hope. You can decide who do you want to be. Rowena McEvoy, the co-founder of Max College, tells a story that goes like this.

Imagine you are out of the house and a detective comes into town with a mission to find out 'who' you are. She has a photograph of you and knows some of the local places you frequent. Armed with the picture and a notebook, the detective visits the petrol station, supermarket, shopping mall and hairdresser you go to and enquires about you. She writes down the words people use to describe you. What do you think they might say?

Next, she goes to your home. As no-one is home, she carefully breaks in. She looks around, looking for clues as to who you are. The detective opens your pantry and fridge and examines the food you eat. Are the dishes left on the bench? Is there rubbish on the floor? Next, she makes her way into your bedroom. Is the bed made? Are your clothes hung up? She looks under the bed, in your closet and notes down the words that describe your habits.

Whist this seems pretty invasive, and it is just a story, it illustrates that who we are in public may be different to who we are in private. Who is the real you? Whatever you answer to this question, stay calm. We are all a work in progress. I can personally vouch for the fact that if you came into my house unannounced, there would be dust on the coffee table, tiny cobwebs in some corners and my teen's shoes and socks left on the lounge room floor!

The point is to take some time and think about who you want to be. What is your ideal identity, your ideal for you?

Over 600 words in the dictionary define a person's positive qualities. Scan a selection of these below.

Circle or highlight the ones you are and the ones you would like to be.

List of Personal Qualities

I am...

Academic	Easy-going	Informal
Accurate	Emotional	Intellectual
Active	Energetic	Intelligent
Adaptable	Fair	Inventive
Adventurous	Far-sighted	Kind
Affectionate	Forceful	Leisurely
Alert	Formal	Light-hearted
Ambitious	Frank	Loyal
Broadminded	Generous	Mature
Business like	Gentle	Methodical
Conservative	Good-natured	Meticulous
Courageous	Healthy	Mild
Curious	Helpful	Moderate
Daring	Honest	Modest
Determined	Humorous	Natural
Dignified	Imaginative	Obliging
Discreet	Independent	Opportunistic
Dominant	Individualistic	Optimistic
Eager	Industrious	Organised

Original	Resourceful	Tenacious
Outgoing	Responsible	Thorough
Painstaking	Retiring	Thoughtful
Patient	Robust	Tolerant
Persevering	Self-controlled	Trusting
Pleasant	Sensible	Trustworthy
Polite	Sincere	Unaffected
Practical	Sociable	Unassuming
Precise	Spontaneous	Understanding
Progressive	Spunky	Uninhibited
Prudent	Stable	Versatile
Purposeful	Steady	Wholesome
Realistic	Strong	Wise
Reflective	Strong-minded	Witty
Relaxed	Tactful	Zany
Reliable	Teachable	

Choose five (yes, you can have six if you must!) words to focus on this year.

Write these on your diary cover, display them on the bathroom mirror, add them to your screen saver. The more you see them and are reminded of who you would like to be, the faster you can develop these qualities.

I go through this process in my depth at my Creating The Life of Your Dreams workshop and webinars, and this process is outlined in my book, *Creating The Life of Your Dreams.*

Setting yourself up for success

The way you start your day can set you up for the rest of your day. This is the central premise behind Robin Sharma's *5 am Club* and many other morning routines.

I have been practising this for over a year now, and it has undoubtedly transformed my life in a multitude of ways. Below is an outline of why a morning routine is essential and the 20/20/20 formula to set yourself up for success each day.

Now, I know, you may be reading this (if you got past the mention of 5 am!) thinking, "there is nothing that would get me up at 5 am", or maybe the thought crossed your mind, "Is there a 5 am, I've never seen it!" I was the same. The thought of extending my already busy, full-on, often exhausting day was not my idea of fun. I read the information and decided to try it for 66 days. I have not looked back and wonder how my life would have looked if I had started this ten years ago. Please suspend judgement and keep reading. This is not a fixed formula, and you can massage it to fit your lifestyle.

Morning routine

A great morning routine can be the bedrock of stability in a constantly changing world. With so many distractions and demands on our time, a morning routine maximises the positive influence you have on your day.

Your brain chemistry is different in the mornings. You wake with an increase of dopamine (the feel good hormone & neurotransmitter) and higher levels of serotonin, which regulates your mood as well as your sleep, appetite, digestion, learning ability, and memory.

You also have the greatest willpower first thing in the morning, which is related to your circadian rhythm. Think of it as a bucket of willpower you receive each day. It is refilled while you are sleeping and is fullest when you wake. This makes important choices and decisions more effortless in the morning, and as the bucket slowly empties each day, it makes decisions harder in the evening. This explains why many people find it easy to eat nutritious food in the mornings and digging into the chocolate chip biscuits by the late afternoon. If you want to change your habits, the morning is the easiest time.

Creating a morning ritual also sets your brain up for success as each time you perform a positive task, you are rewarded with a dopamine surge. Getting up and making your bed straight away gives you a dopamine hit. Doing something to better your life each morning will provide you with that dopamine boost.

While 5 am may still sound out of reach, Jeff Sanders, author of *The 5 am Miracle* says

"Firstly, 5 am is a block of time each morning when life is calm, serene, and peaceful. In the early morning hours, there are few distractions, the birds are just beginning to sing, and life moves at a slower pace. Secondly, 5 am is a symbol for taking full control of your life."

An essential part of developing this peace, focus and clarity in the morning is to leave your phone, emails and social media off until you have finished. These cause instant distraction, using up valuable 'bandwidth in your brain.

The 20/20/20 formula

So what do you do at 5 am? This is a common question I am asked when explaining my morning routine. I enact Robin Sharma's 20/20/20 formula. Known as the 'Victory Hour,' it looks like this.

The first 20 minutes is about exercise to help your body wake up. This is usually something sweaty to decrease any remaining cortisol in the body (the stress and fear hormone) and releases BDNF, brain-derived neurotrophic factor, which grows, repairs and restores brain cells. The second 20 minutes is for what Robin calls heartset & soulset. Take time to reflect, plan, journal, pray, meditate. Anything that helps you to search and find inspiration and purpose. I reflect on what I will do each day to nourish myself, strengthen my relationship with Denny, plan how I will connect fully with my children and plan my top five work goals or tasks for the day. Finally, the third 20 minutes is devoted to learning and growing. This is when I read, listen to a podcast, watch an educational video or TED talk. I genuinely believe that genius is not the realm of genetics. It's the realm of deep study.

Choose something you would like to learn or improve and spend time each day learning about this. As Robin says, "Small daily acts of execution over time lead to stunning results."

As I said at the start, this is not set in concrete. If 5 am is not an option, do it at 6, or 6.30 am. There is something peaceful about 5 am though! It is about carving out time for yourself, making your inner life a priority and doing the deliberate practice. I have found it is OK to miss a day, but not two days in a row. If you are looking for higher focus, better productivity and more fulfilment in your life – give it a go!

> *It is so important to take time for yourself and find clarity. The most important relationship is the one you have with yourself*
>
> -DIANE VON FURSTENBERG

> *If each of us would only sweep our own doorstep, the whole world would be clean.*
>
> —Mother Teresa

CHAPTER 10

MAINTAINING THE RELATIONSHIP WITH YOUR PARTNER

> *A great relationship is about two things. First, appreciating the similarities and second, respecting the differences.*
>
> -UNKNOWN

"Flirting with your husband is weird" This was a friend's comment on my post on social media recently. It made me smile and remember the importance of two things. Firstly, maintaining a loving relationship with your spouse, partner or significant other through the trials of parenting and secondly, the value of role modelling.

If you are solo parenting or sharing the parenting role over two homes, you may wish to skim this chapter although I do believe there is relevant information here for you.

The Language of Love

It was not until I read Gary Chapman's book *Love Languages* that I realised there are different ways to give and receive love. One of the fundamental mismatches between couples is that they offer and receive love differently. (There is a singles version of this information, which is very similar.)

Here is a summary of Gary's 5 Love Languages

1. Words of Affirmation

"If this is your love language, you feel most cared for when your partner is open and expressive in telling you how wonderful they think you are, how much they appreciate you etc."

2. Acts of Service

"If your partner offering to watch the kids so you can go to the gym (or relieving you of some other task) gets your heart going, then this is your love language."

3. Physical Touch (or sometimes called Affection)

"This love language is just as it sounds. A warm hug, a kiss, touch, and sexual intimacy make you feel most loved when this is your love language."

4. Quality Time

"This love language is about being together, fully present and engaged in the activity at hand, no matter how trivial."

5. Gift Giving

"Your partner taking the time to give you a gift can make you feel appreciated."

One way to discover your families love languages is to notice what others do for you. People often give love the same way they like to receive it. Have you ever bought a gift for someone, something you like, and kept it? One of my best friends did!

I visited my friend a few weeks before Christmas. On her table stood a beautiful candelabra. I commented on how beautiful it was. She confessed she had bought it for me. However, she loved it so much she decided to keep it! She did go back to the shop to see if they had another one, but no. (As a side note, if you buy a gift for someone and keep it, don't tell them!)

Love languages are similar to this. Denny shows me love, by touching, cuddling, kissing, and being physically close. I, however, love the little and extraordinary things, a hand-made card, the bed being made, my dinner being cooked- all acts of service. His hands-on approach used to drive me crazy and not in a good way! My nagging about him helping without being asked annoyed him. Now we understand the Love Languages, we are far more compassionate and forgiving towards each other needs.

To explore this concept further, read Gary Chapman's book *Love Languages* or check out his website at www.5lovelanguages.com

Connect each day (overshare warning!)

Many years ago, I was at a conference, and the stunning Lisa McInnes-Smith was talking about maintaining the spark in your relationship. She asked the question, "When was the last time you passionately kissed your significant other?" Too often, in the busyness of life, we get caught up and often give a token peck on the cheek or lips when we leave or come home. I was relating this to Denny, and ever since, he has asked me EVERY single day, "Have you passionately kissed your husband today?" And I do!

Now, this does not have to lead to anything else (unless you want it to), and it has taught me so much. Firstly, it has taught me to take a full 30-60 seconds each day to fulfil his need for intimacy. Second, to do this every day, I have to put aside the gripes and grumpiness I might be holding onto. Thirdly, it has taught me to put everything else aside each day and indeed 'be' with him for that small moment. Not thinking about work, the GST, children or life's challenges. To simply be present in the moment. It has added to our connection and deep love. Thanks, Lisa!

What might be the love languages (we are more than just one) of your significant other, and how might you connect with them every day.

Give to get

> *Work harder on yourself than you do on your job.*
>
> - JIM ROHN

One day the children will leave home, and I certainly do not want to suddenly wonder who this person is that I married is. I want to do everything I can each day to ensure we remain close and best friends. I would add to Jim Rohn's quote above: Work harder on yourself and your primary relationship than you do on your job or your children.

I flirt with Denny regularly. I send him cute texts, leave notes in the shower, wink at him frequently. I have even stopped at his work, walked into a room while he was giving a presentation, blew a kiss across the room and left! Apparently, he turned to his audience and announced, "I have no idea who that was!"

As a couple, we have the mantra, 'have more fun than is allowed!' I often hear people say they wish their partner or significant other were more playful, fun or spontaneous. Please don't wait for them. As the quote attributed to Gandhi states, "Be the change you want to see in the world." When I step into this active role, Denny does too. I regularly receive a dozen red roses via text emojis! After a while, it becomes a habit or second nature. It might feel awkward at the start, and that is OK.

Step up and be the person you would like your partner to be. Remember, it takes time for change to occur for both of you.

I can't mind read!

Talking about and communicating your needs easier said than done.

I was privileged to spend a day with Dr John Gray, the author of *Men are from Mars, Women are from Venus*. He talked about how often in a relationship, especially if you have been together for many years, we expect the other person to mind read. To just know what we are thinking and then act. Well, they can't. John told a beautiful story about his wife, wishing he would buy her flowers. As a subtle signal, she left an empty vase at the top of the stairs.

John walked past and thought, "There is a vase at the top of the stairs." On day two, he noticed two vases at the top of the stairs. By day three, John saw three vases at the top of the stairs and called out to his wife, "Honey, would you like me to throw these vases out?"

Most times, being subtle simply does not work. Quite frankly, I'm sure my husband would not have even seen the vases! LOL. Ask for what you need. If you let your partner know what you like and dislike, plus your expectations, they can meet them so much easier.

The magic fairy

If you have not seen the YouTube clip called Magic Coffee Table, google it. I showed this to Denny, and he 'got it.' We now joke about the magic fairy that does tasks in our house. Usually, it is a comment such as, "I think the magic fairy forgot to come yesterday!" or "I love the way the magic fairy wiped the benches down yesterday." It is a fun and light-hearted way to chat about our expectations, disappointments and praise. It works both ways!

> *The best security blanket a child can have is parents who respect each other.*
>
> -JANE BLAUSTONE

> *Don't let your ice cream melt while you're counting someone else's sprinkles.*
>
> —Akilah Hughes

CHAPTER 11

THE POWER OF GRATITUDE

> *Practicing gratitude brings joy into our lives.*
>
> -Brené Brown

Gratitude is a practice for both you and your children. It is such a game-changer I have dedicated a chapter to it.

Gratitude is the art of being thankful. The word comes from the Latin word gratus, which means pleasing or thankful. It is being able to show appreciation and return the kindness of others. Gratitude is about showing that you don't take life, circumstances and people for granted.

Research by Dr Martin Seligman, known as the father of modern positive psychology, and many other renowned thinkers, show that the practice of gratitude increases people's levels of wellbeing and happiness.

This practice helps people feel more positive emotion, relish a satisfying experience, improve health, help with adversity, and build strong relationships. Gratitude can be shown for the world, a specific individual and yourself. It can be felt and expressed in multiple ways. For example, for the past, by retrieving positive memories, in the present by not taking good fortune for granted and in the future by maintain a hopeful and optimistic attitude.

The benefits of gratitude

A deliberate gratitude practice has been shown to light up the brain's reward centre and flood the frontal cortex with neurotransmitters such as dopamine. This has been shown to spark activity critical to sleep, orgasms, mood regulation and metabolism. Focusing on the positive can shift your heart rate, creating a feeling of stability and calm. Studies show that being grateful can increase social connections and create more satisfaction with family, friends, colleagues, your community and yourself.

Practising gratitude can lessen anxiety and depression symptoms as it challenges negative thought patterns, which calms the anxiousness, and boosts moods. Gratitudians also report an increase in empathy and compassion. The more thankful you are, the more likely you will act positively towards others causing others to feel grateful. It creates a ripple effect.

Gratefulness can also increase resilience as it helps you bounce back from stressful events. Productivity increases due to feeling more inspired and uplifted. It improves physical health by strengthening the immune system, lowering the blood pressure, which, in turn, reduces symptoms of illness.

Ways to cultivate gratitude

> *Feeling gratitude and not expressing it is like wrapping a present and not giving it.*
>
> -William Arthur Ward

The key to cultivating gratitude is a daily practice and not to rush it. You want to stop and feel it deeply. Ideas include:

- write thank-you notes
- thank someone mentally
- keep a gratitude journal
- count your blessings
- pray and/or meditate

Gratitude on the hard days

At a superficial level, gratitude shifts your focus from the negative to the positive. The mind is unable to focus on two thoughts simultaneously. You can't be happy and sad at the same time. The more you train your mind to focus on the positives, the more positives you have!

But what about those days when it is hard? Believe it or not, the best time to practice gratitude is on the days that you don't feel like it. It is not always easy, and it can transform your mind and life.

Podcasters Marc & Angel Chernoff suggest that gratitude can broaden your focus and reverse the tunnel vision of the hard stuff during the tough times in life. They are clear that it is OK to feel the hard times' pain (and essential too), and it is also important to remember the rest of your life. On those more challenging days, Marc & Angel suggest giving these ideas a go:

- Make a list of all people, happenings, events, stuff that you are genuinely grateful for and display it in a place you will see it every day
- When someone upsets you, find one aspect about them you are grateful for
- When procrastinating on a task, be grateful for the opportunity to complete the task
- If you are sick or injured, find thankfulness in being alive and your body's incredible ability to heal
- If someone doesn't like you, be grateful they care enough to give you their attention.

I'd add, make a list of what you love most about your children and display photos of them that bring you positive memories and joy. These are great to go back to on the more challenging days. To see the innocence, joy and pure love from your child and remember they are more than their current behaviour.

The great thing about gratitude is that if you look for it and can't find it, Neuroscientists say it still has a very similar effect in the brain as if you did find things to be thankful for.

> *Gratitude should not be just a reaction to getting what you want, but an all-the-time gratitude, the kind where you notice the little things and where you constantly look for the good, even in the unpleasant situations. Start bringing gratitude to your experiences instead of waiting for a positive experience in order to feel grateful.*
>
> -Marelisa Fabrega

The secret of gratitude

The secret to gratitude is creating a deliberate and sincere practice. Every day, hour, moment, you have the opportunity to choose to be grateful, again and again, and again. It is not always easy, and it is worth it. The effects might not be noticed immediately. Think of it like compounding interest at the bank for your savings account. It takes several weeks or months to start seeing the benefits.

Create visual reminders on sticky notes or download an app (there are many to choose from) to give you a daily prompt. I have a private Facebook group where people post three things a day they are grateful for. You are welcome to join at www.facebook.com/groups/2130234256994390. It is a fantastic community!

Of course, you don't have to believe the research. If you at not sure, try it. It costs nothing, and you just might be pleasantly surprised.

> *Enjoy the little things in life, for one day you may look back and realise they were the big things.*
>
> -Robert Bault

CHAPTER 12

PUTTING IT ALL TOGETHER

Caution! Do not attempt all of these ideas at once. Now you have read this far (thanks for that!), please remember this book was designed as a buffet or a 'pick-n-mix' of ideas that have served my family and maybe ideas that will bring more joy and connection to your family.

Putting new ideas in place takes time. Changing habits takes time. Give new ideas and strategies time.

Set a monthly focused goal

> *To do two things at once, is to do neither.*
>
> -Publilius Syrus

Start with one idea. Just one! Attempting to implement too many things at once is almost guaranteed to fail. Choose one idea, strategy, activity and focus on it for at least thirty days.

I create one monthly challenge and goal for myself on the first of each month. There are two hundred and sixteen months in the first eighteen years of your child's life. Wow! If your child is sixteen, you still have twenty-four months. You have time!

Set a focus for the month. It could be:

- Setting up jobs for your children around the home
- Praising your child when they are responsible
- Doing the no tech challenge
- Starting a National Wagging Day
- Letting go of your perfectionism
- Not rescuing your child when they forget their lunch
- Start a gratitude list
- Give yourself the best chop
- Finding time for yourself each day
- Creating some connection rituals with your partner
- Creating a contract for your adult child living at home
- Starting a morning routine

Start with ONE idea, install it until it is a habit and then add another goal. There may be push back because change is unsettling for many people. Persist, take it slow, adapt the ideas to fit your family and circumstances.

Everything is hard before it is easy

> *To get to easy, you have to go through hard.*

This was a soft drink commercial on the back of buses and billboards in Wellington, New Zealand.

It is easy to look at others achieving their goals and think it is fun and easy. It is not always! Sometimes it is uncomfortable, awkward and that feeling of potential failure is something most of us like to avoid. However, this is precisely what learning new and unfamiliar habits feels like. When learning and life become hard, many people give up. Again, the key is, as the advert says, "To get to easy, you have to go through hard."

Robin Sharma, author of *The 5 am Club: Own Your Morning. Elevate Your Life* shares research from University College London. The research shows it takes 66 days to install long term change into your life. The first 22 days are hard, where you have to let go of the old habits, practices and beliefs. Most people give up during this stage, and the key is to keep going, reset, try again and accept small failures as learning opportunities.

The following 22 days are messy as you create new neuro-pathways. As you are installing the new habit, confusion and exhaustion may set in. You may hear conflicting information, and others may challenge your decision to change your routines and behaviour. I love the idea that obstacles are nothing more than tests designed to measure how seriously you want the rewards!

It then takes a further 22 days to create 'automaticity.' In this last phase, you move from hard to easy, and you know it is becoming a habit when it is easier to do it than not to do it.

The two minute rule

In his book, *Atomic Habits*, James Clear writes about adopting the two-minute rule. He suggests boiling down a new habit or routine into something that takes less than two minutes to do. All habits can be scaled down to a two-minute version that will get you started and help you succeed. James' list includes:

"Read before bed each night" becomes "Read one page." "Do 20 minutes of exercise" becomes "Put my exercise gear on." "Fold the laundry" becomes, "Fold one t-shirt."

Once you get started, momentum will often keep you and your child moving forward.

Final words

> *Life affords no greater responsibility, no greater privilege than the raising of the next generation.*
>
> -C.Everett Koop

Every parent tells me their children are growing up too fast. Mine did. I blinked, and they were 21 and 18. Ask a grandparent, and they are likely to tell you that the reward for parenting is being able to do-over with their grandchildren. To spend more time, enjoy them and not be so serious. I have a mentor who says. "If I'd known how amazing grandkids were, I'd have skipped the children!"

My advice to parents is to have fun, enjoy the ride and know in the good and challenging times, this too shall pass. Practice being a joyous parent. Hide in the cupboard and jump out saying "boo" when they come home (I still do this!), laugh more, connect more and best of all love more.

Create the strong roots of stability with role modelling being a great human and setting up firm boundaries. Teach them to be independent by trusting and slowly letting go, so they have the wings to fly.

You've got this.

> *Success without joy is an empty victory.*
>
> -ROBIN SHARMA

JOYFUL PARENTING

CAMP OUT IN THE BACK YARD   ACT SILLY   CLIMB TREES
Dance in the rain   Have a water balloon fight
Eat the cookie dough   PLAY "THIS LITTLE PIGGY WENT TO MARKET"
Paint each others faces   Go through memory lane by looking at old photos
MAKE IT MAGICAL   LAUGH AT THEIR JOKES   SWING IN A HAMMOCK
HUG OFTEN!   Take turns saying tongue twisters
BE FUN!   THANK YOUR CHILD FOR WHO THEY ARE
Say yes often   Get messy   BUILD PAPER AIRPLANES
Go on a lunch date   Make Mistakes   Soak in your child's stories
EMBRACE THIS TIME   DECORATE THE FOOTPATH WITH CHALK
Fly a kite   Give butterfly kisses   DESIGN A T-SHIRT
Be a pirate for a day   EXERCISE TOGETHER!
Collect shells   Go on a bug safari   Make eye contact
CREATE ART TOGETHER   Tickle   CREATE MUSIC
Play in the rain   JUMP IN PUDDLES   Explore
GO FOR A BUSH WALK   Blow bubbles   Play hide and go seek
Make every moment count!   PLAY PRETEND   Make masks
Read them that extra story   Play horsey
Sing songs   Have picnics in the house
MAKE A FORT WITH BLANKETS   Play in the mud
Make lemonade   Jump on the trampoline
Practice gratitude together   PLAY DRESS UPS
HAVE DANCE PARTIES   Play card games
Play board games   HAVE A WATER PISTOL FIGHT

YOUR CHILDREN WILL BECOME WHO YOU ARE; SO BE WHO YOU WANT THEM TO BE
IF YOU CAN ONLY GIVE YOUR CHILD ONE GIFT – LET IT BE ENTHUSIASM

BONUS CHAPTERS

BONUS
CHAPTER 1

SUPPORTING YOUR TEEN THROUGH EXAM YEARS

If your teen is in their exam years, it can be a very stressful time – for both of you. Exams are not the be-all and end-all for your teen, and these years are a great way to help prepare them for the world of employment in the years ahead. Life can be stressful, overwhelming, and challenging, and learning to handle these situations is essential in growing up. It is also wise to remember that while your child was learning to ride a bike without trainer wheels, they fell off many times before they succeeded, and this may be true of their senior years at school. When your teen was an infant, you encouraged, praised and gently supported their efforts, and the same applies to exam years. The difference is perhaps that you are now taking the role of the guide on the side, the coach, rather than the parent, and allowing them to work through the challenging times with your support.

Here are some tips to support them throughout the year.

Continue the normal routine

Keep everything as normal as possible at home. Ensure they maintain their sport, cultural activities, church commitments or whatever they enjoy doing. Encourage your teen to continue to join in family life and keep up with their weekly chores around the home. This will help them see that the year is just like any other, and the home expectations remain the same.

Discuss expectations

What do exams mean to your teen? Are they a means to the end, a necessary part of schooling, or are they something that they must do their absolute best at? Must they get A's in every subject, or do they just want to get enough to pass? Remember, this is their exam year and not yours! If they choose not to work, that is their problem/learning opportunity. Encourage them and you cannot force them. Help them think through the consequences of their actions and inaction. Personally, our son was clear he didn't want to go to University (and be shouldered with a student loan and a degree he might not ever use.) All the encouragement fell on 'deaf ears', and he did enough to pass, except in his last year. He is now happily employed in a full-time job and loving life. He may continue his learning later on in life when he has a clear purpose and reason.

Give help, but don't control – this is a time for learning self-management skills, learning to learn and personal responsibility.

Know their schedule

Encourage your teen to timetable and plan the year. Their brain is not fully developed until the mid-twenties, and time management is a skill they are probably still growing. Make up a year planner with assessments marked in, alongside their personal activities and commitments. This will help them keep track of what needs to be completed and help the family know when the pressure might be rising. Ensure there is appropriate flexibility within their schedule as things change and opportunities will arise throughout the year. During my exam years, I learned my best time management as I was swimming thirteen times a week and travelling to swim meets most weekends over the summer. I developed strategies that I still implement today.

Know how to study

This might seem obvious, however, it is not for many. There is a massive difference between doing homework in the early years of school and studying. The former is about doing what the teacher has assigned and handing it in for marking. Studying is memorising content and learning what you don't know to pass a test or exam. It is worth pointing out that just because your teen is spending time looking over their notes and books, this 'busy' work may not be an effective way to learn. My 27 study tips can be found by downloading my FREE app iStudyAlarm.

Provide nutritious snacks

Did you know whilst the brain is only 3% of the total body weight, it uses over 20% of the fuel (food) when learning. Learning and studying take energy. Keeping the fridge full of healthy food is a great way to support your teen. Fresh fruit & vegetables, nuts, wholegrain bread, and water are essential for excellent brain focus. Avoid sugary drinks, caffeinated products such as coffee, tea and energy drinks, MSG (often found in 2-minute noodles) and high sugar nut or protein bars. These might cause a temporary spike in energy, resulting in a more significant low and a crash later on.

Create a great learning environment

Your teen needs to have a place that they study. This could be at the kitchen table, a desk and chair in their room, a favourite chair or bean bag etc. Most teens work best with low lighting. Ensure they have the equipment they require, such as coloured markers, notepaper, pens, etc. Not all teens react well to a quiet study zone, and if they are playing music, it is recommended they use music without words or classical Baroque music quietly in the background.

Invite them to 'teach' you

One of the best ways to know you know or have learned something is by teaching or explaining it to others. Saying the information aloud will also reinforce it in your memory. Ask your teen to 'teach' you what they have been learning.

Take frequent breaks

Long periods of study can be detrimental to recall as the brain gets tired and loses focus. Research recommends studying in short bursts, such as 20 minutes on task followed by a 5-minute break. This way, the brain has time to rest and gives time to process it. Download my FREE app iStudyAlarm to assist with this.

Ensure they are sleeping sufficiently

Teens require a surprising amount of sleep to keep their brains at their best. Quality sleep provides both mental and physical rest and is when the brain consolidates the learning from the day. Check your teen's room is dark at night, and there are no blue lights from phones or devices. Any blue light will inhibit the body from making melatonin, the hormone required for regulating our sleep and wake cycles. This includes limiting the use the phones and technology in the bedroom, as they emit blue light.

Maintain your positivity

Be extra aware over the weeks surrounding exams and significant assessments and provide extra grace for crankiness and eye rolls. Study is not always fun and easy – if it were, everyone would do it! Research clearly shows parent stress can harm your teen's performance, which might perpetuate the cycle of anxiety. Maintain your positive support, praise their efforts. Remember, the only control you have is the positive relationship you have with your teen. Be gentle if they fail – we all do, and this is often when the biggest learnings occur.

It is always important to remember that exams do not measure intelligence, kindness, caring, fun, generosity, creativity, people skills, or life readiness beyond school. They measure how much they can remember and recall in a timed, somewhat stressful situation.

BONUS CHAPTER 2

A STUDY SESSION IN ACTION

Recently I helped a Year 11 student with an important test coming up in 2 days. Her parents reported that she has been distracted by a TV show on Netflix and playing a sport, and she had commented that there was no use studying for the human biology test as she would fail anyway. Does this sound familiar in your home? As I was at their house for dinner, I offered to help.

After a tense talk about how capable she is (with her refuting it repeatedly) and that passing requires more effort than intelligence, she begrudgingly started to work with me to learn her biology. Below is the process we started.

Important Note: Two days before the test is NOT enough time to learn the amount of content that she had. Something is better than nothing, and once she got into the flow, she found it was easier than she thought.

1 Decide on where to start

With three weeks of content from a daily lesson at school, there was a great deal of content to recall, so the first step was to decide where to start. Choosing has always been a challenge for this young lady as she does not like to be wrong. However, she finally decided to start with the brain. Here are her notes on the brain from class.

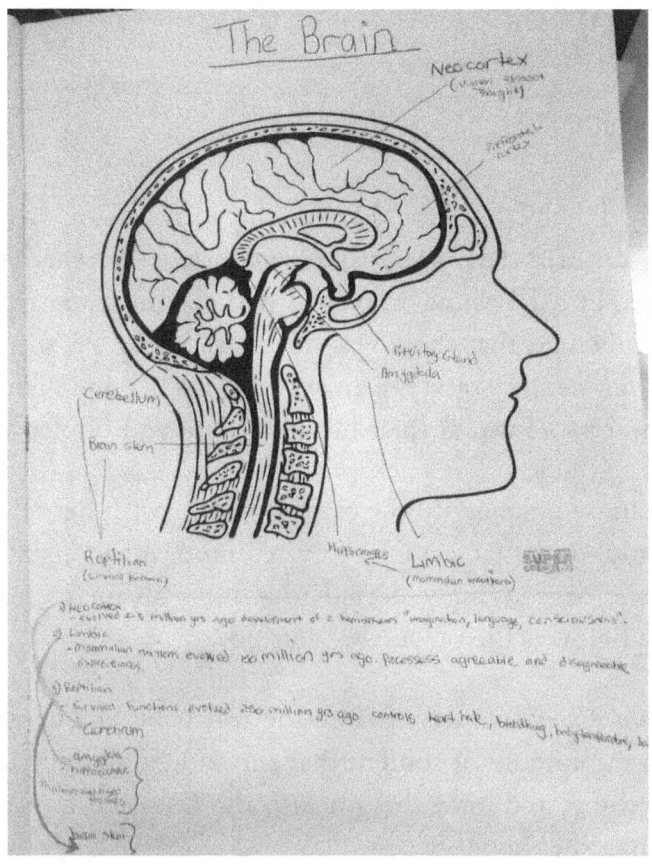

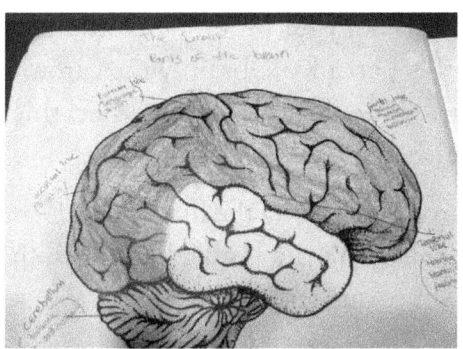

2 Chunk it down

Your short term memory has a limit of being able to recall information. Learn a maximum of 3-4 pieces of information at a time. We took the three main parts of the brain, the Reptilian, Limbic and Neo Cortex and started there.

3. Add actions

Muscle memory is one of the most robust memory systems within the brain. Adding movement to learning enhances the brain's ability to recall. It is vital that the student does the actions and not just the teacher, so the memory is embedded firmly. Here is what we did: We represented these with actions:

> * Reptilian – hold your hand up, close your fist, and release your index finger. This represented the brain stem from the spine up into the head's base.

* Limbic – Wrap your other hand around the index finger to show this part of the brain wraps around the Reptilian with love. (The love indicates that this is the brain's emotional centre.)

* Neo Cortex – releasing the limbic hand – make a sweeping motion over where the limbic hand was, showing the next level, which covers the first two.

We practised and revised this a couple of times, having her say them out loud.

4 Add Visual prompts and further detail

We then drew a brain diagram (not accurately) with the starting letter of keywords as prompts. This developed step by step as she used her notes from class to find the information. She said this aloud, and it sounded like this: "At the base of the brain is the **R**eptilian brain responsible for **S**urvival. It controls your **B**reathing, **H**eart rate, body **T**emperature and **B**alance. Surrounding this is the **L**imbic brain, which is about emotion and our **L**ikes and **D**islikes. Surrounding this is the **N**eo **C**ortex where **T**hinking happens. It is where **Im**agination, **Lang**uage and **C**oncentration happens." While she was speaking this, she was also doing the above actions.

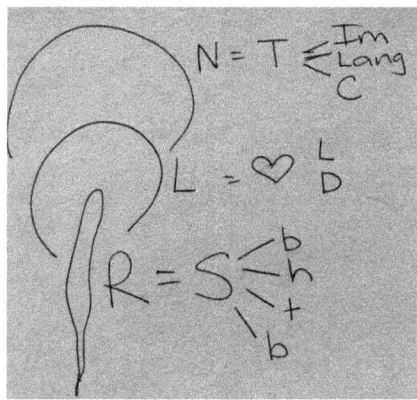

5 Repeat, repeat, repeat

Again she practised this a couple of times with the notes and then turned her notes upside down to see if she could recall the information from memory. This is an important step, as in an exam or test, there are no visual reminders, and it must be from your memory.

6 Tell someone

Talking aloud is a powerful way to learn. Have you ever asked someone to remind you to remember a task you need to do, such as a meeting at 3 pm or to take an item with you when you leave the house? Does that person usually need to remind you? Not usually! Saying it aloud again reinforces it in your memory. At this juncture, I sent her to tell her Dad what she had just learned. It doesn't matter who you tell. Tell your cat, dog or teddy bear! It is about creating another chance to embed the brain's information through another channel.

7 Celebrate the mini successes & take a 5-minute break

We fist pumped each other, and she took a 5-minute break. Learning takes energy as the brain is an energy hog. Frequent breaks are vital.

8 Check you know it and add the next layer

A quick revision to anchor in the success, and we added the next layer:

The Cerebellum is responsible for co-ordination & balance

The Temporal Lobe is responsible for hearing, learning and feeling

Finally, the Parietal Lobe is concerned with language & touch.

A few repetitions with this, and she could recall it without the visual prompt.

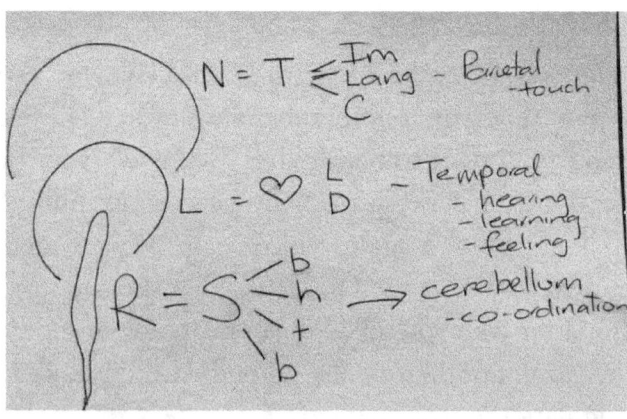

9 Leave the easy until last

Now we needed to add two more: the Frontal and Occipital Lobe. The Frontal Lobe was a quick discussion about what lay behind her forehead and why it was essential to keep this part of your brain safe (not heading a ball in football etc.), and its role in doing complex, complicated problem-solving. The Occipital Lobe (the visual processing centre) was drawn with the O as an eye, and she finished. Adding these more straightforward concepts made it simple to recall at the end.

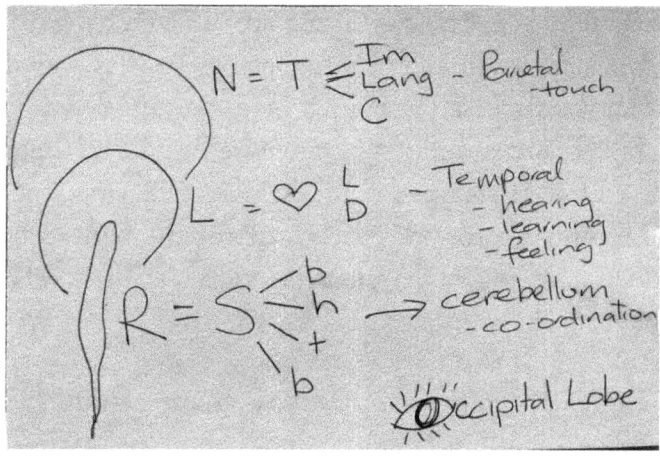

10 More repetition

She spent a couple of minutes revising the information with me and then her Dad.

11 Another break to allow the brain to process and rest

Just like a computer file taking time to download, it also takes time in the brain for information to cement. Frequent small breaks can assist with this. I have developed an app, the iStudy-Alarm, to help keep students focused. It is free to download on all phones (at the time of printing this book.)

12 The next concept

After an extended break and dinner, we did a quick revision and started on a new topic; The nervous system. Laying in front of the fire, we discussed the three main parts to learn: Cranial, Peripheral & Autonomic systems. Tired and still fragile, she made up a little dance like routine (whilst still laying down.) She touched, pointed to or waved the part of the body concerned. This ended up being very amusing, and the laughter was a great welcome from the evening's tenseness.

* Cranial: from the brain to the eyes, ears, mouth, head and spine

* Peripheral: from the spine to the arms & hands, the legs to feet

* Autonomic: From the spine to the lungs, heart, stomach, intestine, bladder and reproductive organs.

13 Revise the next day

As pre-arranged, I rang her the following day, and we took 2 minutes before she left for school to go over what we had learned last night. She had a couple of hesitations and one part she could not recall, so that is the goal for her study next session after school.

14 Refuel and repeat

After school is the time to refuel, rest, and then get back into it with revising yesterday's content, paying specific attention to what she missed in the morning, and then following a similar process for at least two more areas: Heart and Lymphatic systems.

Whilst two days has not been enough time for Miss 15 to learn all she needed to know and understand for this test, I hope it has been an eye-opener for her about her potential and ability to learn and remember. We talked about chunking it down over more days next time and asking for help whenever she needs it.

If your teen requires help with their study, check out our study resources at www.spectrumeducation.com/study-resources

More articles on studying smarter can be found at www.karentuiboyes.com/category/study-skills/

BIBLIOGRAPHY

BIBLIOGRAPHY

Bell, Travis; (2020) *The BucketList Blueprint- 12 steps to #tickit-B4Ukickit.* Dean Publishing, Australia

Boyes, Karen Tui; (2018) *Study Smart – Your Essential Guide to Passing Tests and Exams.* Spectrum Education, NZ

Boyes, Karen Tui; (2019) *Your Weekly Gratitude Focus.* Spectrum Education, NZ

Boyes, Karen Tui; (2020) *Creating The life Of Your Dreams – A step by step guide to vision boarding.* Spectrum Education. New Zealand

Boyes, Karen Tui & Watts, Graham; (2009) *Developing Habits of Mind in Elementary Schools:* An ASCD Action Tool. ASCD, USA

Brown, Margot; (2011). *The 72 Hour Rule: A Do-It-Yourself Couples Therapy Book!* Brown & Brown Enterprises. USA

Carner, Lauren, & Iadavaia-Cox, Anegla; (2012). *Raising Caring, Capable Kids with Habits of Mind.* The Institute For Habits of Mind, USA

Clear, James; (2018) *Atomic Habits - An Easy & Proven Way to Build Good Habits & Break Bad Ones.* Penguin Random House, USA

Chapman, Gary;(1992) *The Five Love Languages: The Secret to Love That Lasts.* Northfield Publishing, USA

Chernoff, M; (2015). *12 Little Known Laws of Gratitude (That Will Change Your Life)* www.marcandangel.com

Costa, Arthur & Kallick, Bena; (2008) *Learning and Leading with Habits of Mind: 16 Essential Characteristics for Success.* ASCD, USA

Coulson, Justin; (2020) *Understanding Discipline.* Interview at Parenting For Resilience, Confidence & Independence Online Summit. www.spectrumeducation.com

Dweck, Carol; (2006) *Mindset: The New Psychology of Success.* Random House

Grant, Adam; (2014) *Give and Take- Why Helping Others Drives Our Success.* Penguin Books

Grose, Michael & Richardson, Jodi; (2019) *Anxious Kids.* Random House. Australia

Lashlie, Celia (2010) *He'll Be OK: Growing Gorgeous Boys Into Good Men.* HarperCollins

Jenson, Eric; (1995) *Super Teaching.* Turning Point Publishing, USA

Medina, John; (2008). *Brain Rules: 12 Principles for Surviving and Thriving at Work, Home, and.* Pear Press, USA

Morrison, Kim, & Whelligan, Fleur; (2002) *Like Chocolate for Women: Indulge and Recharge with Everyday Aromatherapy.* Tandem Press

Morrison, Kim; (2018). *The Art Of Self Love*. Ocean Reeve Publishing, Australia

O'Neil, Lisa; (2020) *Parenting Power.* Interview at Parenting For Resilience, Confidence & Independence Online Summit. www.spectrumeducation.com

Parsons, Lauren; (2015) *The Quality of Your Thoughts Determines the Quality of Your Life.* www.laurenparsonswellbeing.com

Plucker, J & Esping, A; (2014) *Human intelligence: Historical influences, current controversies, teaching resources.* Retrieved 2020, from http://www.intelltheory.com

Siegel, Daniel, & Bryson, Tina; (2011) *The Whole-Brain Child: 12 Revolutionary Strategies to Nurture Your Child's Developing Mind.* Delacorte Press.

Seligman, M. E. P. (2012). *Flourish -A Visionary New Understanding of Happiness and Well-Being.* Atria Books.

Sharma, Robin; (2018) *The 5 AM Club: Own Your Morning. Elevate Your Life.* HarperCollins, UK

Sutton, Kari; (2020) *Raising A Mentally Fit Generation: Science-based tools and strategies to build resilience and wellbeing in our kids.* Karisue Pty Ltd, Australia

APPENDICES

APPENDIX 1

Age-Appropriate* Jobs for Kids

Ages 2-3

- Pick up/put away toys
- Unload the dishwasher (silverware, plastic cups, unbreakable)
- Dusting
- Sweep the floor
- Put clothes in the dirty clothes basket
- Collect dirty clothes
- Help move clothes from washer to dryer
- Put clothes away
- Make bed
- Wipes cabinets

Ages 4-5

- All Previous jobs
- Load the dishwasher
- Vacuum couch

- Take out recycling
- Set table
- Clear table
- Wash dishes (supervised)
- Clean windows
- Wipe out bathroom sinks
- Match socks
- Fold tea dishes
- Gardening
- Water indoor plants
- Feed pets

Ages 6-8

- All previous jobs
- Meal prep (wash procedure, find ingredients, simple cutting)
- Wipe bathroom sinks, counters, toilets
- Hang out laundry
- Sweep
- Vacuum
- Collect rubbish
- Get mail fold/hang laundry

- Clean microwave
- Rake leaves

Ages 9-11

- All previous jobs
- Make simple meals
- Rubbish/recycling
- Wash/dry clothes
- Clean toilets
- Mop floors

Ages 12-14

- All previous jobs
- Clean tub/shower
- Make full meal/meal plan
- Clean out fridge/freezer
- Mow lawn
- Supervise younger children's jobs

* Please take into account your child's specific abilities and maturity level when assigning jobs.

APPENDIX 2

How to Give and Receive an Apology

Giving an apology is a complex social skill which, like all other social skills requires modelling, practice and feedback. Equally there is skill in being able to accept an apology as well.

A good apology has three parts:

1. **"I'm sorry."** Saying sorry can be the hardest part and needs to be genuine rather than forced. Forcing someone to apologise rarely has the desired effect of the person learning the lesson or changing their behaviour. A genuine apology comes with being able to understand the consequences of your actions, how it is perceived by the other person and a degree of empathy.

2. **"It was my fault."** The second step is taking ownership for your actions taken. Admitting you were at fault and taking responsibility. At this stage it is important not to make excuses or blame the other person, as this negates the first step.

> *Never ruin an apology with an excuse.*
>
> -UNKNOWN

3. **"What can I do to make it right?"** The last step is to be accountable for your actions and ask what you can do to fix the situation. Of course if a suggestion is given, then you need to follow up on it and do what you can to correct the situation.

Being on the other end of an apology also requires skill to be able to accept it gracefully, while also not letting the person 'off the hook'. Often the default response is "It's OK" however it was not okay, or an apology would not be required. "It's OK" minimises and trivialises the apology. An acceptance of an apology has 3 parts.

1. **"I appreciate your apology."** This acknowledges that it may have been difficult for the other person to give the apology and conveys your gratitude that the person has made the effort to make amends.

2. **"My feelings were hurt because…"** Step two is to be honest about your emotions and show you are not being casual or flippant about the situation. Be clear and direct about how you felt when the other person behaved badly.

3. **"I accept your apology."** The final step is to accept the apology. You might choose to comment on how you understand why they did what they did and forgive the person. Tell the person you want to continue a positive relationship and move on.

Accepting an apology in no way means your hurt feelings suddenly stop or that you are now best buddies again. It is, however a step towards healing and moving forward.

> *The first to apologise is the bravest. The first to forgive is the strongest. The first to forget is the happiest.*
>
> —Unknown

APPENDIX 3

Questions At The Dinner Table

- ★★★ What three words best describe your day?
- ★★★ What made you smile today?
- Which of your five senses would you least like to give up?
- ★★★ What do children know more about than adults?
- ★★★ If you could go to the Olympics in one sport, which would it be?
- ★★★ What was something you learnt today?
- ★★★ Who inspires you?
- ★★★ What is the colour of the day today?
- What is at the top of your To Do list right now?
- ★★★ What is a great adventure you would like to embark on?
- ★★★ What would you like to change about today?
- ★★★ What is one of your life dreams?
- ★★★ When was the last time you did something for the first time?
- ★★★ What is your favourite thing about this season?
- If you could be anywhere in the world right now, where would you choose?

- ★★★ Which famous living person would you like to have dinner with?
- ★★★ What made you laugh today?
- ★★★ Tomorrow will be better because...
- ★★★ What is your favourite outfit?
- ★★★ If you were a fictional character from a book or film, who would you be?
- ★★★ What kind of trophy would you like to win?
- ★★★ How do you think your grandparents childhood was different from yours?
- ★★★ What is one thing you would like to know about the future?
- ★★★ What would you like to do with your next holiday?
- ★★★ If you could revisit any year in your life, which would it be?
- ★★★ What would be on the menu for your ultimate birthday dinner?

APPENDIX 4

Contract for an Adult Child Living at _____ Household

Between: _____ – and– _____

This contract was set forth on _____ (date) in order to establish terms and conditions ["house rules"] for _____ while living downstairs in this household.

This contract runs from this date till _____ (1-2 years) or prior when the adult child leaves for residence at university or to another living situation. On this date the contract will be reviewed if the adult child is still in residence. In consideration of being provided with room and board, the adult child agrees to the following terms and conditions:

1. **Room and Board Charges:** I am aware that I will be charged for room and board at a reduced rate of $____ per week, as long as I comply with all of the rules below and complete all jobs given to me. If I choose not to complete the jobs that I

have been given then I will pay $____ per week to cover room and board.

2. **Cooking, laundry and jobs:** I agree to complete the following list of jobs in order to help out in the household and to avoid extra room and board charges. I will be responsible for taking my dirty washing, including my sheets and towels once a week, to the laundry for washing. I am also responsible for my own personal space and will keep it orderly. I will be provided cooked meals as long as I help with the cooking, wash dishes and clean up after myself or others when the kitchen is in need of it. Other jobs to avoid paying extra room/board charges include:

   1. Mowing the lawn every week (in spring) or as required
   2. Vacuuming half the upstairs of the house, and my downstairs room and the office area
   3. Cleaning the downstairs bathroom and toilet once a week
   4. Ensuring the downstairs kitchen, microwave and fridge are clean at all times
   5. Emptying the household rubbish bins weekly and putting the bins out ready for Weds morning collection

3. **Guests and quiet hours:** Household quiet hours run from 11:00 p.m. to 7 a.m., unless otherwise arranged. No overnight guests without prior arrangement.

4. **Work:** I will have a job while living in this household. I will do everything in my power to be timely and coordinate rides to my job if need be. If I happen to lose my job or am currently unemployed then I know that I will have 2 weeks to find employment. If I do not find employment within this time period, then my parents will assign me more household duties to help those family members that are working.

5. **Vehicle:** I am responsible for my own petrol and maintenance of any vehicle owned by me. If I cannot afford petrol, I will find rides in some other fashion.

6. **Cell phone:** I will be responsible for paying for all charges associated with my cell phone.

7. **Respect:** I will be respectful to all members of this household. This includes ensuring I say goodbye when I leave the house and come upstairs to say hello when I return. If I am in any way disrespectful to my parents or other members of the household than I may be subjected to fines or extra jobs.

8. **Holiday Fund:** If I wish to participate in the family holidays and activities, I understand I must contribute $50 a month to the Family Bank Account. This covers all adult's birthdays and Christmas gifts and I understand I may buy a small gift,

less than $20, for members of my immediate family for special occasions. I do agree to acknowledge birthdays with a card.

9. **Family Meetings:** If I do not feel that I have breached a term or condition then a family meeting/court will be called, and I can plead my case. The family can then decide whether there has been a breach, and whether any breach is grounds for any fines, additional jobs or imposition of room and board charges. Although I do realise that my family may have a part, it is ultimately up to my parents to decide whether or not I will be subject to any consequences.

My parents reserve the right to change this contract at any time and as a courtesy will give me 5 days' notice before the change takes effect. My parents also reserve the right to make exceptions to these rules at any time, for any reason, at their sole discretion.

If I fail to abide by these rules, my parents can and will take away privileges as appropriate, charge fines or fees.

Son's signature ———————— Date: ————————

Mum's signature ———————— Date: ————————

Dad's signature ———————— Date: ————————

APPENDIX 5

Extra bits I wanted to share!

There are so many extra ideas that others are continually sharing with me and that I couldn't find a place to squeeze into this book. So, I'm popping them here! Random ideas that just might help.

Catch them being good

Remember that children need lots of praise for doing the right thing. Do your best to ignore the negative behaviours and praise suitable actions. You will get more of what you pay attention to.

You have never done this before

I remind myself of a wonderful thought, especially when parenting gets tough; I have never parented a seven-year-old boy before or a sixteen-year-old girl. You are a first-timer and a novice, and it is OK not to know what to do. Even when parenting child two, three or four, you will still encounter new situations and experiences. It is especially acceptable to ask for help, google answers and make it up as you go along.

Read with and to your child

Reading with and to your child sets up wonderful memories and exposes them to incredible rich language, which will give them a head start in school. Language is the basis of thinking. The better a child's language acquisition, the easier learning at school can be. Just one book a day for five years equals 1825 books. That is a considerable amount of language, not to mention quality time for your child. Reading together at bedtime is an excellent way to create deep roots and stability for your child. Plus a love of books, stories and language.

Activities Jar

Another excellent idea for monthly family dates is to start an activities jar. Give each family member several slips of paper and ask them to write one family date idea on each piece of paper. Add the notes into the jar. Each month, draw out a note, and there is your family activity for that month.

Period Blanket

For many girls, getting their first period is either a celebration or something they don't want to talk about. When our daughter started menstruating, I purchased a colourful fluffy blanket and presented it to her. She would use it during 'that time of the month' and return it for washing, ready for the next month. She usually slept on the blanket or wrapped herself with it, or snuggled it. It was a special mother-daughter message (this would be great for Dad's dealing with a menstruating daughter too) which let me know it was that time and helped explain or warn for pending irritable or grumpier than normal behaviour.

Temper Tantrums & Meltdowns

The main difference between a tantrum and a meltdown is that tantrums have a purpose, commonly to change somebody's mind. Children will often check to see if you are watching, and an audience is essential. Once the child has what they want, the tantrum stops. A meltdown is a result of sensory overload. It is a reaction to feeling overloaded or overwhelmed. A child having a meltdown does not require an audience, and there is no goal. The behaviour will stop once they are calmed down.

Tantrums and meltdowns look the same from an outsiders point of view; screaming, kicking, shouting, stomping, swearing, biting etc. How you deal with both situations is different.

Giving in to a tantrum rewards the behaviour as they got what they wanted. A great strategy is to walk away and take the audience away. Meltdowns require loving support and often just being there for your child. Sitting with them and provide only a reassuring presence. Resist talking to them as your voice may add to the overloaded feelings.

After school challenges

After school can be challenging with tears, irritability, and general unhelpful behaviour. It is worth remembering a full day at school can be exhausting for many children. Let's face it, a day at work can be the same for adults! Learning takes an incredible amount of energy, and so does sitting still.

Daniel Siegel and Tina Payne Bryson, in their book *The Whole-Brain Child: 12 Revolutionary Strategies to Nurture Your Child's Developing Mind,* share how talking through a situation might not initially work. They suggest your HALT and ask yourself;

> **H**ungry – is my child hungry?
> **A**ngry - is my child angry?
> **L**onely – is my child lonely?
> **T**ired – is my child tired?

If the answer to any of these four questions is yes, focus on helping them with their basic needs before providing coaching, guidance or advice.

Celebration Jar

This is a great activity to do each year. Find a large jar or a small box that will work, and each time someone in your family has a 'win' or a proud' moment, write the event on a slip of paper and add it to the jar. At the end of the month or year, open the jar and read all the beautiful moments you have shared and celebrate.

School holiday or weekend boredom

My children are super fortunate to have a bedroom full of toys, games and activities. When they would come to me and complain they were bored, I implemented a system that I was then allowed to go into their rooms and take one toy, game or activity and give it to charity. They soon stopped moaning about boredom. I know another parent who has a 'job jar.' When her child complains about boredom, they are invited to randomly select a job from the jar and complete it.

I saw this acronym recently:

> Have you…
>
> > **B**een creative
> > **O**utside play
> > **R**ead a book
> > **E**xercise for 20 minutes
> > **D**one something helpful

APPENDIX 6

Kindness Challenge

You don't need a reason to be kind. Kindness is always a choice. The more you practice it, the more natural it becomes. Practice being kind each day for the next 14 days by choosing 1-4 ideas from the lists below. You can choose from one category or all four each day. Choose your level of kindness. Add your own ideas as well...

KINDNESS to SELF
- Do something that makes you happy today
- Exercise for 10 minutes and get your heart pumping
- Smile more often
- Avoid complaining for the entire day
- Create a new game and play it with friends and family
- Take time to practice mindfulness
- Take long slow deep breaths for 3 minutes
- Listen to your favourite music

KINDNESS to FAMILY
- Help with the chores without being asked
- Express your gratitude to your family
- Play a game with a family member
- Wash Mum or Dad's car
- Make a handmade card for someone in your family
- Tidy up after yourself
- Surprise a family member by doing their job for them
- Cook a meal
- Leave a special note on a family member's pillow

KINDNESS to OTHERS
- Write a letter or note to someone out of town and post it
- Bake a cake or your favourite food and deliver it to a friend or someone in need
- Find opportunities to give compliments today
- Say "thank-you" as much as possible
- Hold the door open for the person behind you
- Do something kind for a stranger
- Greet people with a Hug, High Five or Handshake

KINDNESS to PLANET
- Use less plastic
- Drink from a reusable water bottle
- Turn off the lights when you leave the room
- Use reusable shopping bags
- Pick up 5 pieces of litter
- Walk more, drive less
- Recycle
- Make a piece of art work from recycled materials

spectrumeducation

APPENDIX 7

Holiday Acivity Grid

Weekly Activity Grid

© www.spectrumeducation.com

During the week, see how many of the activities you can do. Colour the grid square to show the activities you have completed.

Help set the table for dinner every night	Have a picnic on your lawn or lounge room floor	Read a story to a family member	Draw your family tree
Make a wind chime from recycled materials	Write a letter to someone you have not seen lately	Help clean up after dinner	Collect some fallen leaves from the garden and make a piece of art with them
Play a board game with a family member	Create a family portrait	Make an outdoors obstacle course and time yourself doing it	Have a dance party
Cook a family favourite recipe	Make your bed everyday for a week	Make a phone or video call to a family member	Change the words of a song and video yourself singing it

APPENDIX 8

Alternative Questions to ask after school.

- What was the best thing that happened at school today?
- Who did you play with today that you've never played with before?
- Tell me one thing you learned today?
- If I called your teacher today, what would they say about you?
- Where is the coolest place at the school?
- Tell me a new word you heard today?
- How did you help someone today?
- How did someone help you today?
- When were you happiest today?
- What was your favourite part of your day?
- Did you raise your hand in class today?
- Did anyone vomit today?
- Were you able to finish all of your work today?
- Who is the friendliest person in your class?
- Was there anything that made you sad today?
- Did you do anything you that you don't enjoy today? Why don't you like it?
- Tell me something that made you laugh today?

GRATITUDE & THANKS

This book has been a vision for so long, and I am truly grateful for all the people behind the scenes.

Firstly, to my parents, Tui and Trevor. You have always been available, a listening ear and a tremendous support. You gave me the deep roots of stability and the independence to fly. Because of you, I am who I am. I will never be able to express my gratitude and appreciation fully. Thanks.

To every parent, teacher, principal and mentor who have shared ideas to make my parenting journey joyful and fulfilling – thanks.

To Travis Bell and Rowena McEvoy for your kind permission to add a small piece of your wisdom into this book.

To Marion Miller, Megan Gallagher, Lynley Marwick, Kirsten Reid, Stacey McEwan & Christine Keno for your editing work on the manuscript and my design team, Saravanan Ponnaiyan and Farhan Ahmad – as always, you make my words look so beautiful on the page. Thanks.

To the current and past team at Spectrum, thanks and gratitude for all the help, advice, feedback and new learning and insights.

You are a fantastic group of people focused on our goal of being At The Heart of Teaching and Learning. Thanks for believing in my vision and keeping everything ticking while I wrote.

To my children, my rainbows and sunshine, Hamish & Sasha. Thanks for being my best teachers, reflecting the good, the bad and the ugly, allowing me to grow. You are both fantastic souls and have your whole adult life ahead of you. I'm super proud to watch you develop your wings and take on life's challenges.

Finally, and best of all, to my amazing co-parent, Denny. The shared experience is something so special, and I am eternally grateful to have you by my side on our parenting journey. It has not always been plain sailing, and it has been worth it. Your support, sounding board ears and eyes, editing, and always being there for me with open arms and those sparkly blue eyes is genuinely appreciated and valued. I love you.

STAY IN TOUCH WITH KAREN

Karen loves meeting parents and keeping in touch. To subscribe to Karen's updates and articles please email the Spectrum Education Team info@spectrumeducation.com

To read Karen's latest articles please go to www.karentuiboyes.com/blog

You can find out more about the events Spectrum Education and Karen are hosting, including the FREE Parenting for Resilience, Confidence & Independence Online Summit at www.spectrumeducation.com/events

To invite Karen to speak (in person or virtually) at your school parent meetings, event, summit of conference please email the team at info@spectrumeducation.com

You can email Karen direct at karen@spectrumeducation.com

OTHER BOOKS AND RESOURCES BY KAREN TUI BOYES

Parenting Inspirations Quote Book

Study Smart Book (revised edition)
Study Smart Flip Books
Study Smart Board Game
iStudyAlarm app

Your Weekly Gratitude Focus
Creating the Life of Your Dreams

Project Genius: Big Learning For Young Geniuses
Developing Habits of Mind in Elementary School

Available at www.spectrumeducation.com

www.ingramcontent.com/pod-product-compliance
Lightning Source LLC
Chambersburg PA
CBHW070559010526
44118CB00012B/1383